UNTOLD
RESILIENCE

Stories of courage,
survival and love
from women who
have gone before

FutureWomen

Edited by Helen McCabe
and Jamila Rizvi

This book contains accounts of personal trauma, including domestic abuse and suicide. If any of these accounts affect you, or you or someone you know needs help, you can contact the following organisations:
Beyond Blue: 1300 22 4636
Lifeline: 13 11 14
1800RESPECT: 1800 737 732

PENGUIN LIFE

UK | USA | Canada | Ireland | Australia
India | New Zealand | South Africa | China

Penguin Life is part of the Penguin Random House group of companies whose addresses can be found at global.penguinrandomhouse.com.

Penguin
Random House
Australia

First published by Penguin Life, 2020

Copyright © Future Women, 2020

The moral right of the authors has been asserted.

Cover design by Patti Andrews, Future Women
Text design by Midland Typesetters, Australia
Typeset in Georgia by Midland Typesetters, Australia

Printed and bound in Australia by Griffin Press, part of Ovato, an accredited ISO ANZ/NZS 14001 Environmental Management Systems printer

 A catalogue record for this book is available from the National Library of Australia

ISBN 978 1 76104 015 3

penguin.com.au

*In memory of the grandmothers whose advice
we miss so much,
Margaret 'Peg' Bowes and Queenie McCabe; and of
Lakshmi Maksay, who died shortly after sharing
her extraordinary story with Future Women.*

*And dedicated to the nineteen women who opened their lives,
hearts and memories to us.*

Contents

Introduction

By Jamila Rizvi, Future Women

'For young people who have never been through any of those things, or lived in a time when they were happening, this seems just frightful ... But if you've witnessed, heard about and know people who've been through these other things, you think, "Well, we're going to make it through this."'
– Margaret Atwood

It was Booker Prize-winning author and international treasure Margaret Atwood who did it. It was her fault I found myself sitting on the bathroom floor with my back against the door (to block my insistent four-year-old from entering). I'd been listening to her speak on the popular *Dear Sugar* podcast when she said the words inscribed above. In that moment, my previously stalwart efforts to avoid giving in to pandemic grief began to fail. I sat there beside the toilet, my poor old bum soaking in the coldness of the tiles, and sobbed until there was nothing left inside.

My coronavirus isolation happened hard and fast. The night before, I'd been at a Future Women event full of smart, diverse and very funny women. While guests had avoided the standard hug-and-kiss greeting, the room was still absolutely packed.

This was a sell-out crowd. There were more than 250 people in the audience, each sitting quietly side by side, captivated by the speakers on stage. We were moved and humbled. Now, when I think about that audience's prolonged proximity to one another, I cringe.

The next day, my husband and I made the decision to bunker down. I have a series of chronic conditions that make me particularly vulnerable to illness. In the early days when people were casually saying things like, 'It's only sick and old people who will die from the coronavirus,' I was one of those whose death was apparently acceptable. I needed to stay safe and, for that to happen, my family needed to keep themselves safe as well. We agreed that over the weekend we'd make the necessary preparations to self-isolate, suspecting that everyone would be joining us sooner or later.

And then my husband got sick.

It is a truth universally acknowledged that nobody experiences a cold quite like a man, and the one I married embodies this cliché. But this was no ordinary seasonal sneeze-fest. Jeremy had a high temperature, chills and a horribly sore throat. He had shortness of breath, aches and pains in his limbs and the most horrendous-sounding wet, rasping cough.

In the early days of the pandemic the criteria for testing was tight, unlike now. Australia didn't have enough tests to go around and we didn't know how bad the situation was going to get. Despite multiple visits to the doctor, Jeremy never qualified for the infamous nasal swab.

And so, our pandemic plan went into action earlier than anticipated. My son was away with his grandmother at the beach and we asked if he could stay there. We didn't want either of them exposed. Not seeing our little boy for weeks was genuinely tough. Jeremy stopped leaving the house at all and confined himself to our bedroom. I started sleeping in another room and left the house only occasionally, in search of caffeine, groceries and Codral. Every waking minute that I wasn't working or on FaceTime to my son was spent cleaning. I sterilised everything Jeremy touched. I was like the lady on the Spray n' Wipe advertisement, who just *loves* scrubbing things until they sparkle. Bleach became my best mate.

Jeremy recovered slowly, though even after four weeks this fit and healthy man in his thirties still got puffed walking up the stairs. We'll probably never know whether the coronavirus arrived in our home in March 2020 but thankfully nobody else in the family got sick. In the meantime, of course, the entire nation had been sent home. New restrictions were declared and updated repeatedly, and fines for breaking the rules increased. A national cabinet was formed, stimulus packages were announced and workers were laid off. Far fewer people left their homes to go to work. Neighbourhoods felt eerie and empty, despite kids being pulled out of school. Oh, and everyone started hoarding toilet paper.

During the ensuing months, a terrifying global picture was painted in real time on our smartphones and laptops. We no longer waited for the nightly news because updates were urgent and often. We felt nervous whenever alerts sounded on our phones and yet we compulsively read every new story that appeared, desperate for the next morbid update. We watched as people died around the world. First China, then Italy, then South Korea, the USA, and then ... everywhere. Hundreds of thousands of lives lost. Many died without access to the health care that might have saved them. At home in Australia, unemployment figures were climbing steadily. Each meagre percentage point represented hundreds of thousands of real people and their families.

I was one of the lucky ones. While money got tighter in some ways, savings were made because we no longer went anywhere or did what we'd usually do. The household remained financially secure and we were physically safe. Family and friends experienced a different and more frightening new normal where changed economic circumstances left them questioning how they'd get by. Loved ones on the other side of the world faced the confronting reality of attending virtual funerals and wondering who might die next. People living in developing countries or housed in close proximity in refugee camps had little to no chance of being able to physically distance. How do you prevent spread when there is one water source for every 20,000 people and soap is a rarity?

I'm a somewhat anxious person. My mum calls me a worrier. But I suspect that I found isolation easier than I otherwise might have because previous illness had left me stuck at home for long periods of time. Despite being a ferocious extrovert, I was used to the slower and quieter pace of life. I was busy with work, I felt safe in my home and well, *who was I to be upset and struggling?* I wonder if you felt the same. Almost as if you were unworthy of fear and panic when there were others doing it far tougher. It's a strange sort of grief: anxiety over an undetermined future, and your heart hurting for people you would never, and now will never, meet.

From the outset of the pandemic, I wanted to speak to my nan. Her name was Margaret Mary Bowes, but everyone had known her as Peg. A mother of three children, and grandmother to nine, Nan's life was shaped by the times she lived in. She was a clever child who skipped lots of grades and won scholarships. Mathematics was her speciality. She could run off times tables up to and beyond fifteen and worked in metrology during the war, which involved measurement and calibration. After getting married Nan had to give up her job, but found work in a post office for a time. Once she had children, family became – and remained – her number one priority.

Nan set off to university later in life, determined to get a degree because she was 'sick of staying home and looking at gum trees'. Graduating in her sixties, she said the hardest thing about her arts degree was finding her car in the packed parking lot after classes. She was always grateful to Prime Minister Gough Whitlam for her free education. I remember Nan as a ferocious reader, incredible cook, impeccable sewer and kind in that no-nonsense sort of way that women of her era tended to be. Women who'd lived through more difficult times.

My memories are understandably of the later years of my Nan's life. Born in 1924, she was a child of the Depression and lived through World War II. In hospital, during the final weeks of her life, she told me horror stories of the polio and tuberculosis pandemics. She was forced to spend many months at home to stay safe and was devastated to miss out on school. In the days before her death, she was as sharp as ever, railing against anti-vaccination proponents. 'They don't know what it was like,' she explained to me, sipping the evening glass of Scotch that's apparently mandatory in a hospice.

Nan died in 2013. Before MERS, the Ebola breakout of 2014 and of course, before COVID-19. In those self-indulgent minutes spent on the bathroom floor in the middle of March 2020, I desperately tried to draw on her wisdom and resilience. I wanted her assurance that people had survived worse and we would survive this too. I imagined Nan's firm but warm voice telling me that despite the present terror, and future terrors that likely lay ahead, we'd be all right in the end. It's a perspective that comes only from having been there before – the kind of perspective Margaret Atwood described.

I needed a compass of personal fortitude, someone who could give me direction and perspective in the midst of this bewildering global crisis that threatened to swallow my sensibility entirely. There were so many 'what if's, not just for me and the people I cared about but for humanity as a whole. The problem felt so inconceivably large, and with no 'end' in sight I was losing my grip on what was real and what was not. When the President of the United States is suggesting their citizens drink bleach while others are dying on stretchers outside of hospitals, realism seems rather relative. Were we really living in a disaster movie? I wanted someone sensible – someone who had been here before – to tell me I should relax and that humans have survived worse.

When Helen McCabe founded the digital platform Future Women, she wanted its membership to reflect an attitude, not an age. Meeting and talking to the incredible women whose stories are contained in these pages has made me understand what Helen meant. Occasionally these incredible individuals' experiences have felt like something from another world, not simply another time or another country. Some of them have survived the impossible. And yet, I felt a shared spirit with the women we interviewed, and a sense of common values.

We could have been close girlfriends had we been born into the same generation, I'm sure. I both admired and felt kinship with them. Future Women is privileged to share the love and wisdom of these women – their lives and lessons – with a new generation. All of you.

The work of collecting these stories has been deeply personal for both the journalists and their interview subjects. The continued dangers posed by the coronavirus pandemic, particularly for older people, has meant none of our journalists could meet face to face with the women whose stories they were telling. At first we were hesitant to embark on such an ambitious project, the success of which hinged on trust and honesty between storytellers. We needn't have worried. Despite distance, age gaps and varied life experiences, our journalists each formed a devoted bond with the women whose stories are contained within these pages. Personally, I cannot wait until I'm able to hold the hands and look into the eyes of the women who so generously shared their lives with me – and say a sincere thank you.

Before now, several of these remarkable women have only ever told their stories through the prism of the men in their lives. Indeed, there were moments when our interviewers found themselves struggling to draw out the stories of the women themselves, and not the men they had loved. History celebrates the brave wins and noble losses of men, but rarely pays mind to the sometimes quieter, intelligent determination of women; women who were fighting courageously for their survival at the same time, in different ways. This book makes a small contribution to setting that skewed presentation of history right. It pays homage to the extraordinary experiences of women who sought no medals and who gave no aggrandising speeches. These are women who put their heads down and got the job done, proving their strength through the steadfastness of their actions.

I cannot wait for you to meet them.

'Be patient. Things will improve. This will pass, just as other pandemics have. It's about being there for yourself too, and knowing what you can and can't control . . . So long as you have family and friends, you should be all right.'

Colleen Hickman

I come from a line of determined women. We are all strong-minded and resilient, with a steady work ethic. My grandmother taught my mother, who then taught me, that you have to work for what you want in life. They used to say, 'You're not any better than anyone else, Colleen, but you're also as good as anyone else.' That advice held me in good stead. I could always tell myself that I was capable of doing things. I was fortunate to grow up in a stable, loving home. I always felt safe and protected, which is why I don't remember many of the effects of the war. This grounding gave me self-confidence and self-worth. I had the skills to deal with any dramas that came my way.

I took on responsibilities from an early age, such as babysitting the neighbours' children and leaving school to go to work very young. I was not ambitious for a career. I wanted a happy home and loving family – which is what I achieved. My understanding of resilience has changed as I have aged. As I've faced bigger hurdles, I have come through because of my belief that things will get better. Now I am in my eighties and I do feel more vulnerable, especially when it comes to health. I can get overwhelmed. The future is less certain for me but I remain a 'glass half full' person and I have wonderful support.

I was nine years old when I contracted diphtheria. We knew about the illnesses children could get, like scarlet fever, tuberculosis, polio and diphtheria. But still, it was the sort of thing you never expected to happen to you. Back then we didn't have vaccines. When I first complained of feeling unwell, my mother accused me of putting it on so I could get out of school. Like anyone else, she didn't think it would happen to her daughter. I had a sore throat and a fever, as well as generally feeling wretched. I was taken away from my home in a van when I was first moved to the hospital. They fumigated the house after I left. I felt very scared leaving my family. Then I was told that I couldn't be with them or even have a visit, and I was devastated.

At the hospital, the nurses would bathe me in something they called phenyl, which was very unpleasant. I remember exactly what it was like to lie in that bath. I hated it. They would swab our noses and throats – like they're doing now to test for COVID-19. We had to have chest X-rays to make sure we didn't have tuberculosis. I didn't ask my parents a lot of questions because it wasn't the 'done' thing at the time. I didn't understand a lot of what was happening to me. I was lonely. They had toys for us at the hospital and I would read to pass the time. I always had a book in my hand. My aunt sent me a parcel full of Violet Crumbles and that's basically my only good memory of it all. The illness left a heavy mark on me. I was probably in isolation for a month, which felt like a very long time at that age.

Before then, I had been relatively untouched by tragedy. I enjoyed a happy childhood, despite the war. My sister Patty was six years older than me and that was quite a gap. When I was ten, she was a teenager and didn't really want me to hang around her and her friends. We had contrasting personalities. Mum and Dad treated us differently. Patty was strong-willed, so our parents were stricter with her. They made her stay at school longer and were firmer with her about her social life and comings and goings. We loved each other and became much closer as adults. Patty only died a few years ago, which meant that we were able to go through life together. For that, I am very grateful.

I was born a few years before Australia went to war, which meant I was ten years old when World War II ended. During the war, I wore a medal around my neck with my name on it, but not because I had won any awards. It served as my identification if we had to go into an air raid shelter. All the school children living in Adelaide at the time wore one. We often had blackouts in the city. We had to block out all the light from the windows in our home, so the enemy wouldn't see us if they ever flew overhead. As a child, I found those times more exciting than frightening. My father was a blackout warden, which meant he was in charge of coordinating the blackouts. That made me proud.

I attended a convent school, which had mixed classes up until grade three and only girls from then on. I loved to play tennis and to run. I liked the nuns, though they seemed terrifying to me sometimes. They were tough, which I respected. The nuns used to cane us occasionally but I think we probably deserved it. As a child I felt the nuns had a certain mystique about them and, as such, they were to be respected and obeyed. I always thought of the nuns and the clergy as being separate to everyone else, like they were somehow better. It was a shock to find out when I was older that they are ordinary human beings with personal lives.

My dad was a footballer for West Adelaide and that helped my parents get through life. They survived the Great Depression because my father had that stable, well-paid position on the football team. There was a strong sense of community back then. Kids would play in the streets more freely than they do these days. We lived in a row of little cottages, which are now heritage listed. We knew all our neighbours. It made us feel like we really belonged. I had a lot of friends too. If we were going to get something down at the shops, we'd always drop by the neighbours and check if they wanted anything. I was aware, even as a kid, of the kindness in the community.

I did love school but when I turned fourteen I became restless. My best friend had already started work and I decided to do the same. I wanted to get out into the real world. I suppose I was in a hurry. My first job was as an usherette at the theatre. It was a glamorous job and I loved film stars. I lied and put my age up by three years. I always looked older than I was and it must have worked because I was given the job. Earning my own money gave me independence, something that has always been important to me. I worked in the booking office, handling money and balancing the day's takings. This was how I developed my love for a challenge and a desire to prove to myself that I can do whatever I set my mind to do.

Both before and after we were married, my husband, Darrel, worked part-time as an usher at the theatre too. Darrel would tell me, much later on, about a time when a newsreel played footage of two soldiers helping a guy with a blindfold on: someone who had obviously been injured or blinded in the war. A woman in the audience stood up and yelled, 'That's my son! My son!' Those newsreels of bombs dropping in Europe and our Aussie soldiers going off to war really affected people. It made them realise how real and how horrifying war could be. For a lot of Australians, that was the first and possibly only time we actually saw footage from the war. We barely knew the truth of it back home.

I started ballroom dancing lessons when I was fifteen. There would be a dance for young people every Saturday. That's where I met Darrel. He was twenty-one and I was fifteen, so he said he'd wait for me to grow up a bit. We didn't get married for another four years, which was a long time back then. If I'm honest, I don't know that I ever really did grow up. In some ways, I still feel like a girl. Many of my thoughts and attitudes haven't changed. I love spending time with younger people and I'm interested in what they do and think. My body has aged and I get frustrated when I can't do the things I want to do, like gardening and vacuuming. I do try to keep fit. Up until eighteen months ago, I was still ballroom dancing weekly.

Darrel and I got married when I was nineteen and I had my firstborn, Cheryl, just one year later. Gail, Kerry-Jane and David followed over the next fourteen years. Having a child at the tender age of nineteen suited me fine because it was like having the most beautiful doll to dress up and play with. I loved being a mother. I've always been maternal. Parents need to be active role models and expect their children to take on responsibilities. Darrel and I must have done something right as our children have all grown into responsible and resilient people and so have their children in turn. A lot of that has been because we are a strong, united family.

I wanted to go back to work after becoming a mother. My husband wasn't overly happy about it because back then men generally thought it was their role to support the family while the wife stayed at home with the kids. But I knew that I wanted certain things, and I wanted to earn money to buy them for myself. My mother had always worked. She was a tailoress who sewed uniforms for soldiers during the war. When the war was over she kept sewing to earn money for extras like the children's dance and elocution lessons. Inspired by her, I wanted to do the same. When Cheryl was two and a half, I went back to work part time at the theatre. My kids have benefitted from my example.

We moved to Melbourne in 1970. It was a big decision to leave our family and friends and our home in Adelaide, but we thought we would be able to offer the kids more opportunities in Melbourne. More sadness was to follow, however, when Darrel had a heart attack at age forty-three. We still had three kids at school and a little one at home. It was traumatic for all of us. In the 1980s, just as we were back on our feet, we got badly hit financially as interest rates went sky-high. By then, Darrel had started his own auto accessories business and he was shot during a hold-up at the store. I was with my dying mother back in Adelaide when it happened. Darrel was closing the shop for the night when someone came in with a gun and demanded the money from his till. It was a horrendously difficult time and everything seemed to have gone wrong at once.

Darrel only survived because the bullet ricocheted off his shoulder and missed his heart by centimetres. It punctured his lung and got lodged in his spine, where it stayed until the day he died. Darrel was often in pain afterwards. I could tell as much, though he rarely complained. His business suffered, but friends stepped in to help while he couldn't work.

There have been hard times in my life, for sure, and I got through them because I am strong. I stand on my own two feet and I look after the people I love. It's about having the right attitude and the right people around you. I'd been with my husband sixty-three years when he died peacefully in his sleep. I had a wonderful husband and, truthfully, life with him was good.

Of course Darrel's death was hard for me, but I try to stay as positive as possible. It's important to remain optimistic. I used to say to the kids, 'You can fall down, but it's how you get up that matters.' I now have six grandchildren and four great-grandchildren, and I want to pass my self-belief down to them. Everything is an experience and to be honest, I've been lucky to come out of so many in my life. Last year I found a lump on my neck, which turned out to be cancerous. I only finished my chemotherapy in February 2020, just before the pandemic hit Australia. I'm a fighter. I've been through six rounds of chemotherapy now. My children rallied around me and I got the all-clear in March. I'm just waiting for my hair to grow back now.

I have been worried about the younger ones during the coronavirus outbreak as I feel they have information overload, with social media and television. We are hearing about many deaths overseas. It must be frightening for people who haven't dealt with something like this before. At first the younger ones thought this was an old person's problem but now younger people are dying from this virus too.

I would say to people who are frustrated or scared: listen to the advice of the professionals and don't overwhelm yourself with the media reports. Be patient. Things will improve. This will pass, just as other pandemics have. It's about being there for yourself too, and knowing what you can and can't control. Stay optimistic and look after your relationships. So long as you have family and friends, you should be all right.

Since we've all been relegated to the house through this COVID-19 scare, I've been reading a lot. Rather like I did in hospital as a child all those years ago. I have my family and friends on FaceTime and Messenger. I speak to them often. Some of my children live nearby and I see them when I can. In normal circumstances, we have lunch together every Wednesday and go shopping. There's only a twenty-year age difference between me and my eldest daughter. We've always felt more like girl-friends than mother and child. We are close and we support one another. I haven't made a lot of money in my life, but I've always had a first-class family. I can't wait till I can go out to lunch with my daughters again. Maybe followed by a little outing to the shops.

Colleen Hickman is eighty-five years old and lives in Edithvale, Victoria. Colleen shared her story with Kate Leaver.

'Resilience in life means having no self-pity. None of that "Why me?" stuff. Nobody is born entitled to a trouble-free life, and there's no supernatural power picking us out for either good or ill luck ... You do learn in the end to live with tragedy.'

Val Reilly

There is no such thing these days as a nurse who can put on a wrinkle-free bottom sheet. But that absence of wrinkles was terribly important for nursing tuberculosis patients. People were in bed for months, sometimes years, so one of the major problems was bedsores and we had to be so careful with the sheets. There couldn't be even the sign of a wrinkle or crease.

There were four of us Melbourne girls who nursed tuberculosis patients together. We were exacting, and our patients were grateful for that. For some years I stayed in touch with people I nursed. If you create that bond of trust, you don't throw it away. Shared experience, and particularly shared ideals, are the glue of friendship, and these are more likely to be shared with fellow females. During years of struggle, talking through our difficulties helped to clarify for us how best to handle them, and often reinforced our determination.

My three friends and I decided that we wanted to be trained up properly – as nurses, not just aides. Considering the quality of the various sisters we worked under, we agreed that New Zealand was the way to go for the best training. Also, to us, New Zealand wasn't really another country; just our neighbours across the ditch. We had our places in Wellington Hospital booked, along with our sea passages to leave Australia, and six weeks to wait for our departure. As it turned out, in those six weeks, all four of us met the blokes we would marry and none of us ended up going . . .

I had several weeks' holiday each year from being a nurses' aide and had taken an alternative job in the city for one of those periods. This was mostly so I could spend more time training as a ballroom dancer, which was one of my hobbies. Unfortunately, the owner of the dance school was getting more interested in me than I was comfortable with. One evening, I ducked out quickly to get a tram home before the owner could offer to drive me. While I was waiting at the tram stop, a car pulled up and the driver said, 'You're a student at the dance school, would you like a lift?' I assumed he must have been connected to the school so I got in the car.

His name was Kevin. Oh, how we talked and talked. We talked until breakfast time, pretty much, and he was extremely charming. Kevin was a panelbeater and a lonely sort of fellow. I would find out later that he had been hurt and abused as a child, which perhaps accounted for his loneliness. I fell for him, of course. I thought I could help him. My saviour complex is something I have tried to inoculate my children and grand-children against, with varying degrees of success.

Kevin and I were married in 1956 at St John's, East

Melbourne. When I got married, I used the petticoats I had worn beneath my ballroom dresses under the wedding dress that I had made. There were layers and layers of green tulle under a pale-yellow waltz-length dress. The Dior 'New Look' had come in back in 1948, while I was still at boarding school. The look was to create a real hourglass figure with whopping great full circle skirts, lots of petticoats and tight little waists with the smallest of belts. During the war and for some time after, women's magazines gave regular space to articles on how to alter clothes or improvise. My sister and I had been well taught by our mother, so we knew how to make our own clothes.

Well, it was a great wedding – and a shit marriage. Kevin and I had our honeymoon in Geelong and within a couple of days I'd had the first of the beatings that would continue throughout our marriage. I thought of leaving many times in the years that followed but I had been taught that marriage was 'indissoluble'. In those days I'd also have been destined to live alone and child-less if I had ended my marriage. Later, of course, those same children were a barrier to financial survival if I were to leave. Fear of beatings became a constant in my life and because I was a well-brought-up Catholic girl, I did not complain. I did not tell anyone what was happening. I thought, *Well, this is it now. I will have to get used to it. I've made my bed, now I must lie in it* . . .

My parents were also young when they got married. Neither had reached the age of twenty-one when I was born in 1934, at the height of the Great Depression. My earliest memories are of living with my mother's parents on a bush block with nothing 'laid on'. Our light was from kerosene lamps or candles and we collected rainwater in tanks. There was a well in the backyard, but if it ran dry, I would help my Nana carry buckets filled from the creek. We would put water in the copper to heat up for the washing or to fill a bath. I still regard it as the epitome of civilisation to step under a shower, turn on a tap and have the water at the exact temperature that you choose.

One set of my grandparents gifted my parents a block of land in Mansfield and they were given a house by the other. By the time I was four years old, we were living there, with my father's parents 400 metres away from us, over the creek. You had to cross the creek via a wooden plank to visit them. It was an adventure. Because I was the eldest of what would eventually be eight children, I was often sent to run messages across the plank, with the water rushing below. We were poor but we weren't desperate. We had our own land and our own animals. We made our own butter. Our family had no luxuries, but we had enough. During wartime rationing, we would pool the tea coupons and give them to my grandmother because that was her only luxury. It didn't really feel like hardship because everyone was doing it.

The war started in September 1939, when we were living in Mansfield. At the time I had no real idea what 'war' meant. We were country kids and far more protected than our city brethren. At one stage we were digging air raid shelters for no reason, just because we were kids and we'd heard of other people doing it. I gradually got the picture of what war was about when I started reading the paper aloud to my dad. He had poor eyesight because of eye injuries when he was young, so one of my tasks was to read to him when he asked. The only newspaper my family could afford was the *Weekly Times*, but Dad also subscribed to parliamentary Hansard because he was interested in politics.

I can still recognise the names of politicians whose speeches I was reading way back then.

A contribution we did make to the war effort was to save fat and send it to Britain. It was either mutton fat or beef dripping, and we had plenty because we 'killed our own'. When a certain amount had been saved it would be 'clarified' by further cooking and put into a large tin. I think it was the Red Cross who would then send it to our hungry British brethren. We would also use that fat to make our own laundry soap – bought soap, such as Velvet, was a luxury.

At one stage a young airman came to visit my dad. He had been one of those responsible for dropping bombs on Dresden, as I recall. I remember him saying how difficult it was to think of the real people down there: he was trained to think of them only as targets but, of course, he realised that he was killing innocent women and children. I can still see his face now, see his little tremble as he spoke about that. It was truly painful for him and his visit really brought the reality of war home to us, in our protected country life.

As I grew older, I got to know that war also meant ships being sunk and lots of casualties. I couldn't comprehend that word 'casualty' as a child but eventually came to understand. While my mother was pregnant with twins, I lived with my grandmother and went to a little one-teacher school where we had to give a 'morning observation'. On one occasion, mine was that the HMAS *Canberra* had been sunk as part of the war. My teacher was surprised because mostly we would report on grasses or birds or animals, the usual things country children noticed. This little school had only ten students, so there were activities going on at several levels, for different ages. I tuned in. I don't recall ever being told to stick to my level; my curiosity was simply accepted.

Apart from this, my siblings and I went to a 'convent' school, and many of us students were idealists and believers in self-sacrifice. Perhaps that's why I decided to join the Sisters of Mercy, which meant going to Geelong to a terrific place called Stella Maris Juniorate. It was like a boarding school for girls wanting to join up. That's how I got my secondary education, ending with matriculation before I had even turned seventeen. I had three very happy years in North Geelong and made friendships I still have today. One of these friends, still a Sister of Mercy, remains very precious to me. 'Friends since 1946,' she will still tell new acquaintances.

I never actually made it into the Sisters of Mercy, however. I had a bit of a row with Mother General. She told me that I would probably find Obedience – one took vows of Poverty, Chastity and Obedience – quite difficult and should take some time to think about it.

Time drifted on and I became a nurse's aide for tuberculosis patients, working at Greenvale Sanatorium. By that time, the Australian government had started a mass compulsory chest X-ray regime to screen for tuberculosis. I arrived at Greenvale just as they were introducing the best drugs there had ever been for tuberculosis. Initially we were caring for patients who were skin and bones, barely able to sit up and expected to die. Full bed rest and lots of fresh air was the only treatment. As nursing aides, we were not even supposed to make the poor buggers laugh because their lungs were so fragile. I used to think that was probably worse for them psychologically. But with the new drugs, in a few months those same patients were able to walk out. It was miraculous. The government's main tactic had been to catch the disease in the community and to compulsorily treat it. There were no restrictions on where people could go or what they could do, as there have been with the coronavirus.

Our nursing uniforms were cotton cesarine: a straight green button-through, with white buttons and collar, and a wide starched belt. It wasn't particularly fitted but it looked all right. We also wore a starched white cap. Those uniforms were boiled a couple of times a week to guard against the spread of illness and make sure they were always fresh. Hair had to be up, not down around our shoulders. Otherwise our hair would have been another thing hanging around ready to pick up germs. Very different from current hospital practice – stuff dangling from lanyards would have been unthinkable.

We were carefully trained in barrier nursing and taught to avert our faces, so as never to take in the breath of other people. We learned to wash patients completely and do just about every-thing for them while following that particular directive. The floors were washable and scrubbable, not carpeted like they are in some hospitals today. The curtains around the beds were con-stantly changed and boiled. Hygiene standards were extremely high and so I wasn't scared of getting sick with tuberculosis, not in the slightest. It might have been ignorance or youth, but it mostly never occurred to me.

It took me a while, with this coronavirus outbreak, to understand a virus as distinct from the bacteria involved with tuberculosis. Hence the need for physical distancing and the emphasis on thorough, frequent handwashing. Those of us who have lived through various other epidemics remind one another that science will eventually find a vaccine. This too will pass.

Though I do worry about healthcare workers, and hope they have fundamentally re-trained themselves in the currently required techniques. When my paramedic granddaughter describes their equipment and procedures to me, I think that very likely these actually make her and other healthcare workers safer than the ordinary citizen.

My children have been a source of enormous comfort and pride. I had my first baby, Daughn, eighteen months after I married Kevin. Then fifteen months after that I had Eva. Eleven months after that I had Gabrielle and fifteen months after that I had Julie. Three and a half years between the birth of the eldest and the birth of the youngest, which was a bit of a challenge, to say the least. Especially because I was trying to manage this overgrown spoilt child of a man who was likely to blow up at any excuse. On one occasion there was a row about whether to have sausages instead of chops for dinner. Kevin had this fifteen-shot .22 rifle that he used to go hunting with. He calmly loaded up all fifteen bullets, getting ready to shoot the lot of us. God knows how I managed to talk him down.

The terms 'domestic violence' or 'family violence' were not in use then. Men were described as 'wife-beaters' sometimes but, in general, nobody interfered. When I did end up talking to the police once, the reactions were varied. 'Don't be silly, he's a friend of mine.' 'We hate these domestics because the charges always get withdrawn before it gets to court.' It was a long time before I heard of protection orders. In Deniliquin, where we were living by that stage, there were several neighbours and friends with children of a similar age. We would help each other by childminding, shopping, sewing for each other or doing hair. Perhaps friends suspected how things were for me and the children, but I certainly never confided in them. I knew that to let 'it' be known would be the end of my respectable façade.

There was a movie around that time called *A Letter to Three Wives*. In it, the three wife characters were told of some irregularity that made their marriages invalid. How I fantasised about such an irregularity that would set me free! If I was okay with the church and the law, I reckoned I'd somehow manage the financial survival of leaving my husband. That movie-based dream was somehow less guilt-making than me speculating on Kevin suffering some fatal accident.

I had put up with violence for six years and it was having an impact on the kids that I could no longer ignore. I may have had a right to sacrifice myself, but I had no right to sacrifice them. After the rifle incident, I was not just exhausted and constantly terrified but desperate, and for the first time I admitted the state of affairs to my family. So my father, my brother and one of my brothers-in-law came up with a big truck and somehow kept Kevin calm while they packed up the kids and me with the absolute minimum of stuff. My dad brought us back to our home in Mansfield, where there were already several of my younger siblings, the youngest being some twenty months older than my eldest child. We were all crammed in there briefly. But one brilliant morning I woke up and realised I was not afraid. The Catholic Welfare Association found us an empty old boarding house in Warburton. It was July when we moved there and it was absolutely freezing.

We were poor, but not conspicuously worse off than the rest of the community. We managed to get by. Things were different in those days. We walked everywhere and could catch the bus occasionally. We later lived in Yarra Junction, where bread was delivered to the door, and groceries too. I can't think now how I ordered or paid for them. I also had a deal with the butcher. He knew I could only afford to spend a certain amount and so he would distribute the money across whatever was cheap at the time and deliver it. That was enormously helpful and that local community was one of the reasons we were able to survive.

In those days, Warburton was the headquarters of the Seventh-day Adventists, who own Sanitarium, makers of Weet-Bix. There was a Weet-Bix factory in town, and I don't know what we would have done if we had not had access to Weet-Bix. For almost nothing you could get a whopping great paper bag of broken bits. The kids didn't know the difference. They would have them for breakfast, yes, but also, they would have them when they got home from school with some butter or honey or peanut butter. It was a lifesaver.

We became a team, the girls and myself. We made decisions together. I tried not to be authoritarian or to use negative orders. My philosophy about child-rearing was that you let go a little bit every day. Children arrive totally helpless and totally dependent and as they grow you let them make as many decisions as they can, so long as it doesn't bring harm to them or do real damage. I wanted my kids to be honest, compassionate, generous and respectful of differences. I hoped they would not hold grudges but appreciate that forgiveness breeds contentment. I wanted them to be self-reliant and use their skills for the betterment of humankind. I suppose that period of poverty, combined with my frugal childhood, did shape who I am. I can't bear waste and still use things till they fall apart.

The most revolutionary advance for women in my lifetime has been effective contraception and the invention of the pill.

I was still too brainwashed to consider using it when I was younger, but its effect has been unimaginably liberating for so many others. Once women were no longer tied to the cradle and the kitchen and were free to earn a living for themselves, the tyranny of marriage was breached; slowly, independence became possible. There's a long way to go before equality of pay, conditions and opportunity is achieved, but compared with the 1950s it's bliss. If only the young ones could realise how hard-fought the battles were to get them the 'privileges' they take for granted and could so easily lose.

Despite earlier hardships in my life, by far the biggest thing I have ever had to deal with was the death of my daughter, Eva. She took her own life as a result of mental illness. Eva was my second child, born on the birthday of my paternal grandmother, for whom she was named. As a baby she was undemanding, and though her milestones were pretty normal, she was never as robust as the other three. She was the only one I sent to kindergarten, as I felt she needed something that was special for her, and for which she did not have to compete with my other children. As an adult nursing aide, her jobs were mostly in aged care, and at times in mental health. Once working, Eva struggled to establish a 'home' of her own, though she was always welcome back with us if it got too hard.

When Eva began to get ill, I had no idea what was happening, not the slightest idea about delusions, bipolar disorder or schizophrenia. I knew things were not quite right with her but didn't know what to do about it. While I was dithering over this, a couple of weeks before the wedding of my eldest daughter Daughn, Eva had an episode. She sat in a café not knowing where she was, and couldn't be persuaded to leave at closing time, so the police were called. The last photo I have of the four girls and me is at Daughn's wedding. There is Eva, sitting beside the others, looking as if she doesn't know where she is. I'm not strong enough to describe the period from then until her fatal overdose . . .

Eva's death has remained there, in the background of my life, and at times it has been very difficult. To me, resilience in life means having no self-pity. None of that 'Why me?' stuff. Nobody is born entitled to a trouble-free life, and there's no supernatural power picking us out for either good or ill luck. It's up to us to play the cards we are dealt. You do learn in the end to live with tragedy. It doesn't ever go away. There isn't a day Eva doesn't come into my mind for some reason or another. Her gravestone says, 'Our dear, gentle daughter and sister.' Shit happens, and when it does, you face it, deal with it, and get on with it. That's been my motto.

Val Reilly is eighty-six years old and lives in Melbourne. Val shared her story with Jamila Rizvi.

'That feeling of having no control must have stuck with me because my adult life has been about finding my voice, so I can play my part in shaping our community. It hasn't been easy.'

Dottie Hobson

When I talk to our old people I realise how much of blackfella history has been about having change forced on us by the white people. Of having to learn to adapt to the new life they wanted for us. I am a Kuuku Ya'u woman and for the first nine years of my life I lived at Lockhart River Old Site. It was beautiful remote country, right on the beach on the east coast of Queensland's Cape York Peninsula. We were happy there until the government forced us to move out. Nobody asked our community what we wanted to do, or how we felt about leaving our home where our ancestors are buried in the cemetery.

We lost a part of who we are – our language, our way of living, our guiding lights of respect and sharing – when we were moved. We were given no choice. That feeling of having no control must have stuck with me because my adult life has been about finding my voice, so I can play my part in shaping our community. It hasn't been easy. I used to be so shy. I couldn't stand up in front of people and speak my mind. That would have been impossible for me. I have had to change and I am proud of the leader I have become. Now there is hope for the road ahead and for the future of my people.

The Lockhart River Mission was set up in 1924 by Anglican missionaries. Clans from five different Aboriginal territories, including Mum's, had been moved from their land to live together in one place. There was no consultation; no one talked to the clan elders, except to say that it was compulsory. Looking back I can see it was about control. In the new mission, people were banned from speaking their own language or carrying out their traditional cultural practices. So much has been lost from that time. Instead there was church – which we learned to love and which remains important to me and my family now.

My dad spoke Kuuku Ya'u. When we listen to other communities who speak their language so well, like in the remote Indigenous community of Aurukun, where everyone speaks the native language, I feel as if something is missing inside me. There is a hole that can't be filled. The old people say that when the missionaries came, they said we shouldn't be speaking our language but should speak English instead. All the clans' languages were banned. After that, between each other, we would speak creole, which is a mix of a pidgin English and some words from the old languages. I am sad that I can't speak my own language. You need to grow up with a language for it to live on. When the old people pass, it will fade out completely.

My grandparents and parents learned to live with the new rules. They were all from different tribes and had been pulled together into a community. There was no way out. Everyone had to get on, and so they did. I remember there was a lot of dancing, and sharing was a big thing. If you went out and got a pig, you would share it with other people too, not just keep it for your family.

I was born in 1960 at the Old Mission, or the Old Site, as we now call it. I was number three of five children. I had two elder brothers, Paul and Philip, who have since sadly passed away, and two younger sisters, Bella and Ivy, who are with me now in Lockhart River. I can't remember too much about the Old Site but I do remember there was a lot of dancing and a lot of church. Church brought us together. Everybody went, every Sunday. Old people, young people, children, babies. It was a place of joy and worship and caring for each other and it was well attended.

Our home was pretty basic: made of bark and right on the beach. I would open my eyes in the morning and there was the lovely sea and the beach and all the seagulls flying around making a noise. We used to play on the sand with other kids. There was lots of swimming and collecting shells and making up our own games. Later, Mum and Dad would go fishing and we would go with them, walking along the beach and catching fish for dinner. Then we would have dinner at home. These are vivid memories for me of beautiful, simple days with everyone together.

We had one bedroom for us kids. Mum and Dad slept in the dining room. Our toilet was a thunderbox in the backyard, literally a hole with a cover over it. There was no electricity at all, we just had lamps, and no running water. Every few days my dad had to go out in the tractor to the river with a 44-gallon drum to collect our water. It was a huge task and would take all day. Dad would growl at us, 'Don't waste the water.' One day my brother got in trouble because he was playing in the water and my dad chased after him. He was so cross.

My brother wasn't the only one who was naughty. Me and my friends were walking to school along the beach and the waves looked so inviting that one day, instead of going to school, we jumped into the refreshing sea water. We had a Torres Strait Islander school principal and I remember he came down and started screaming at us: 'What are you girls doing in the water? Come on, out. You need to come to school!' I was ashamed because I knew I wasn't doing the right thing and I can recall that feeling even today. I was taught to respect my elders and those in authority. Has this served me well? I wonder. These days, I still have respect but I also question authority when I need to.

All of a sudden, in 1969, we had to move. I now know that the Anglican Church handed over the Old Site to the Queensland government to run, and the government decided we must all move to a new place inland, closer to the airstrip. It was part of an assimilation policy, to try to fit us into the government's plans. I was too small to be involved in any of the meetings but I can remember the old people were talking about it a lot and they were crying. Dad was sad because his parents were in the cemetery at the Old Site. He was one of those who stood up and tried to fight, but it didn't work. A couple of people stayed for a little while at the Old Site but eventually everyone had to move.

The government didn't listen to the old people back then. They thought they knew what was best for us and didn't ask our elders what they wanted; they just told them what to do. There was no respect. That move really affected the old people. They were born at the Old Site and grew up there. The traditional owners of that land felt so sad at leaving their country. Ancestral land means a great deal to my people. It is part of us and it connects us spiritually to our people. Actually, this New Site was also my mob, Kuuku Ya'u, land. But back then it wasn't really recognised as such because native title wasn't given until 2009.

My dad and the young fellas had to go and clear the new area, cutting back the cane, because it wasn't prepared. We had two weeks to move. Mum and Dad seemed lost when they said to us, 'Pack up your things, we're going.' I was standing there thinking, 'Going to where?' Mum explained that we had to take everything. She said, 'Look around and make sure we don't leave anything behind.' We were going for good. I saw the sadness in my mum, especially on the day we left. She loved fishing at the Old Site, and living on the beach was part of her identity. I could sense her unhappiness in the way she talked, and even though I was only young I remember feeling so sorry for Mum.

We moved by boat: Mum, Dad, us siblings, my uncle and my aunty. It was a big dinghy with an outboard motor that Dad drove. Our things went on another boat. For everybody else at the Old Site there was all sorts of transport, including a big navy boat that took a lot of families. Some went in their own small boats and others drove overland. The New Site felt very different to our home. When we arrived, there were proper houses made out of brick or concrete and there was running water. The toilets were still in a shed in the backyard. Flushing toilets came later on, along with electricity. But having running water, that was a big relief, especially for my mum.

We were lucky and had a three-bedroom house. At first there weren't enough houses for everyone, so some families had to live in tents. The new house was clean and spacious but we were sand beach people. We desperately missed the water. Our food changed as well. At the Old Site we had bananas and pumpkins, watermelon and lots of fish and seafood. At the New Site there were tomatoes, cabbages, lettuce, but not the fruits I grew up with. There were so many firsts for us. There were a lot of white people around who were building the school. It was the first time we'd seen that many white people. After a while there was a store, though it was very expensive. We had never had a shop before; we had lived off the land and other supplies used to come in by road or boat.

The really big change – which devastated our people – was the canteen. Other Aboriginal communities had one, and so the old people back then said we should get one too. For the first time we had alcohol in our community. There was no education about what alcohol does to you, or the health implications. No one knew what happened if you drank too much and what would happen when you got old. That canteen really changed us because soon there was a lot of drinking going on – including by Dad, who would pay dearly for it later. When I was old enough I joined in. I loved to be down at the canteen at five o'clock, as soon as it opened. I became an alcoholic in my young days. Everybody else was doing it so I thought, *Why not join the bloody club?* My mum didn't drink or smoke, and would tell us to leave the alcohol alone. We refused. We thought we knew everything back then. Alcohol is now banned in Lockhart River but the genie is out of the bottle.

Dad was diagnosed with cancer in 1989. The doctor said it was too far gone and there was nothing he could do. Dad was sent home to die. Even though I had known he was unwell, it was a shock. I remember Mum called us children together to tell us and we were really sad. Mum looked after him at home and Dad got sicker and sicker. The cancer doesn't wait around.

I was at home on the day Dad left us, just a couple of months after his diagnosis. He was lying on a mattress on the floor and Mum said, 'I think he's going to go.' It was very emotional for me, watching my dad die. I couldn't believe that he had gone so soon. It felt wrong somehow.

School was another challenge. We had a better school built at the New Site and our old teacher was replaced. White teachers came in. We had to speak English rather than creole because the white teachers couldn't understand us. Lessons were in English. Looking back, I think it was a good thing to connect us to the rest of Australia but it was another aspect of our culture that was lost. As we got to high school age, everyone was sent away to boarding school. I went to All Souls St Gabriels School in Charters Towers and later to another school in Atherton in the Tablelands. I felt very lonely at first. I had come from a classroom full of black kids and now I was in a classroom full of mostly white kids. I didn't like it. I felt we were treated as different. Other Aboriginal kids had grown up in the city and they were used to it. When you come from an isolated community, it's not so easy. I missed my family and I wanted to come home. So I did.

I was seventeen when I left school and started work in the post office and the bank in Lockhart River. I also got married and, following a couple of miscarriages, I had my daughter Deanka. She was premature but she survived. I have raised three kids in total; Richard was the eldest, who we adopted from my husband's family, then Deanka, and then Grant, who we adopted from Mum's side of the family. Having kids changed me. I had little ones to look after and so I gave up drinking, just like that. 'Cold turkey', as white people would say. I had the willpower to do it, spurred on by my mum and the negative role model of my dad, who was an alcoholic before he died.

Lockhart River New Site was run by the government and we didn't have community people to speak for us. Decisions were forced on us. Then, in 1985, the Lockhart River community elected five councillors to constitute an autonomous Lockhart River Aboriginal Council. I remember the first time we had a blackfella speak at a public meeting and not a white person. We were so used to a white person getting up and telling us what to do that this was a really big thing for us. A woman called Denise Hagan, who used to work for the Queensland government, moved into our community. She set up the Puuya Foundation, which gave us a body to identify our community's needs. Denise showed me that not all white people were against us. She respected and understood our community.

Denise would bring all the women in our community, and those from outside who wanted to help, together to talk. We call it yarning. We would share our stories about how we had each worked through difficult times. As a younger person, I was listening to it all and learning from their experiences. Denise then put me through a women's leadership course to go out to cities to meet with other women. I think sharing your wisdom with other women makes you think the right way and helps you move forward. It gave me a broader outlook on the work that needed to be done in Lockhart River and the best way to achieve results.

The first time I won a place on the council, there were a lot of things that I didn't know. I was told, 'You are a councillor and this is what you have to do.' It was a bit scary at first, but I watched and learned. My education and time on the council really did bring the shyness out of me. I could never speak up for myself before then and I certainly never stood up. I can do it now. I'm confident in myself. Council work became very important to me. People came to me as a councillor. They'd not be happy about something or they'd need me to talk for them. It made me feel good, being able to help our people. In the past we were never given a space to talk; we didn't know how and the white people wouldn't make room for us. Now I can jump in whenever I need to. I tell them, 'Excuse me, I've got things to say.'

My parents taught me that if you know something's not right, you must speak up. If you're not happy, don't keep it to yourself, tell us. It took me time to realise I needed to use that advice in a bigger way, to push harder for the good of my people. We have had losses as a community but we have also gained much: most importantly, control of our shire and re-establishment of our culture. Now we run our council and we negotiate with the government. We are also building our culture. We have a world-renowned group of artists; I paint and make craft jewellery and we have weekly music and dancing led by our elders.

I have had a lot of female role models in my life. Denise helped me become a leader, a woman named Veronica Piva has guided me in the church movement, and Mum taught me to be a good person. Thankfully, women have more opportunities now than in my mum and my grandmother's days. Back then it was only men running things. I was appointed Chairlady of the council in 1994. Being a female leader was a bit difficult at first. I was ignored so often. I think finally women have the same rights as men in our community. The men are listening to us and we are on the same level now. They can't ignore us any longer.

I am now Deputy Mayor of Lockhart River and Chair of the Puuya Foundation, which is dedicated to developing everyday leaders. The Foundation has established our Kuunchi Kakana Centre for early learning, to guide and support our little ones and their parents. Along with the other leaders in my community, we are trying to lead the next generation. We are going to mentor them and show them how it's done. After all, we're not going to be up there forever. One day they will take over. I want to be a role model for my grandchildren and all the children in our community; and the lessons I want to pass on are about the importance of education, being a truly good person in heart and deed, and respecting others.

I have a dream to go all the way to parliament in Canberra, to speak for my people at national forums. Change doesn't always have to be bad. I am going to be part of what happens next, and it feels good.

Dottie Hobson is sixty-two years old and lives in Lockhart River, Queensland. Dottie shared her story with Juliet Rieden.

*'We can accept that, at the moment,
things aren't easy but then we need to
ready ourselves to face events as they
are. There will be different stages in
the growth of every human being, and
this is one of those instances where
something externally imposed will
challenge us all to cope.'*

Lakshmi Maksay

The big, formative influence on my life has been my father. He was a feminist and, for a man of his time, had progressive views. He brought me up to believe that women were equal and there's nothing we couldn't do. My father taught me that I should determine my own life. For a man born in 1897, that is quite remarkable. My father was from a Southern Indian farming community and as a child was sent to a Lutheran boarding school. School was a two-day-plus journey from home. He was such a little boy to be travelling this great distance every six months. My grandfather, who was only semi-literate, was ambitious for the future and had wanted to give his son a sound education.

Being the only son in a family of eight girls shaped my father's life. His sisters were all victims of child marriage. They were each wed around the age of ten or eleven, and made to wait until they reached puberty before going to live with their husbands. Many of the husbands died of smallpox before that could happen. It was a time of pandemics in India and smallpox was raging. Women like my aunties, who lost their husbands before puberty, were called 'virgin widows'. They could never marry again. Some were thrown out of their childhood homes, while others were sent to live with their dead husband's family. My grandfather believed his daughters should live in *his* house. This was highly unusual and that's how the home my father grew up in became known as 'the house of widows'.

My father saw his sisters' suffering and the limitations of their lives. He felt for them. His education and exposure to Western ideas helped shape his thinking as well. He came to the conclusion that to improve a woman's life, it is important for her to be educated and economically independent. My sisters and I were emancipated in that sense. My father taught us that it's not what society decides *for* you, it's what you take on and decide *for yourself*. Later, after my father met my mother and got married, it was his 'bad luck' to have six daughters of his own. Daughters were considered a financial burden. My father often quoted a proverb, which he vehemently disagreed with:

To be blind and to have daughters is a very similar situation. You feel helpless.

He was determined to break with conformist society because of his experiences growing up. Those experiences coloured his whole outlook on life, particularly regarding the role of women. My father wanted more for his daughters, and we benefited immensely. With all that education, my father was not content to live in such a small town. He made his escape to the big city of Madras and then to Bombay (now Mumbai). He wanted to explore. My father was determined to educate us and wouldn't arrange any of our marriages. He said that women should be economically independent. Of course, my parents got a lot of flack for us being unmarried, for sending us to university, and for allowing us to enjoy our freedom. But they believed that we could handle our lives, and that kind of confidence was the best thing that my sisters and I could get.

I had an interesting childhood. I was born a few days after World War II was declared, which, no doubt, caused my parents a bit of anxiety. My father was working for a Scottish company that was responsible for organising air raid precautions in Bombay. When his big boss was asked to select someone to work under him during the war years, my father became that person. That was when our family moved into our new home, the Bluestone House. The Bluestone House was huge. Half of it was a storeroom for equipment to keep Bombay safe from German attack. In that house, there was a lot of talk about the war. My father would read newspapers aloud to my mother and, though I was young, I became aware there were things happening *outside*.

After the war, my father's boss was awarded an Order of the British Empire and he made sure to point out that a lot of the work had been done by my father. My father was given a Silver Medal for Meritorious Service to the British Empire. I remember that day clearly because on the way home we got sweet delicacies to celebrate the special occasion. The end of the war meant we had to leave the beautiful Bluestone House, and finding accommodation in Bombay at that time was a challenge. Suddenly, the city had changed. As a result of the Partition, there were droves of displaced people and refugees. I heard a lot of horror stories about Hindus and Sikhs escaping Pakistan, and Muslims moving back there who thought, 'Oh, I can't live here anymore.'

I have one memory of a little girl who joined my school and was about my age. Her hair was absolutely white. She was subdued and kept to herself. I later found out that she had witnessed her father, mother and sister being shot dead. She ran away, hid under the bed and was the only survivor. Almost overnight, her hair turned white. *How tragic*, I thought at the time. *What kind of experience must that have been*? We encountered a lot of people like her, who came to Bombay absolutely penniless and carrying scars of the past. Those same people were courageous and plucky, so in no time they turned their fortunes around. They made Bombay even more successful through the enterprising nature of the newcomer. Bombay had a sense of possibility about it. Things were also changing for women; we were beginning to find something for ourselves. Bombay post-independence was a place of possibilities for a young woman like me.

There I was, a twenty-seven-year-old woman with a master's degree in English literature and a teaching degree too. I was working at Bombay University but I wanted to travel. I wanted to get out and go far away from where I had grown up. One day I was walking in the centre of Bombay when I wandered past the Australian High Commission building. I went in and said, 'How does one get to Australia?' The woman working at the desk said, 'Oh no, it's very difficult. You can't just go there like that.' I suppose I knew this. The White Australia Policy was still in force back then. I had a university colleague who came back from the war via Queensland because his boat couldn't go directly to Bombay. The boat waited for eight days in Australia but no coloured person, no dark-skinned person, was allowed to leave that ship. Australia had a bad reputation, as the kind of place that shut its doors.

The woman at the High Commission said to me, 'You can't go to Australia unless you have work. Do you have work?' I replied, 'No, I don't have work. How do I get work?' She said, indifferently, 'Look at one of those books over there.' I picked up one of the books and flipped through it, and saw something about Australia needing teachers. It mentioned an Independent Teachers Association, so I took down the address. I've never done anything more casual in my life. On my way back to the railway station, I stopped off at the post office and bought an aerogram. I handwrote it – I didn't even bother trying to make it look good! I wrote that I had all these qualifications, and could they give me some advice on how to go about things. *It's only an aerogram I'm spending money on,* I said to myself.

Two weeks later, I had a letter from Australia! I thought it would say, 'Sorry we can't help you.' But there was a job for me in Echuca, a country town in Victoria, and they asked if I would take it. I got such a shock. I had to get my visa quickly, which was a challenge because the High Commission in Bombay was being difficult. They told me that whoever was offering me this job needed to understand that I couldn't get there for at least a year. But I was determined. I sent another letter to the school, telling them about the situation. A short time later, I got a cable asking me to turn up at the High Commission. The commissioner said that he didn't know what was going on in Australia, but he was supposed to process my application straight away.

Within three weeks I had to resign from my other job and say all of my goodbyes.

I later found out that Echuca's local member of parliament, John McEwen, was the acting prime minister. The principal of the school had asked him to help. And so, out of the tragic circumstances of Harold Holt's disappearance, I managed to get my visa. After I arrived in Australia, John McEwen wanted to know how everything had worked out. I had afternoon tea with him at his country property. It was a lovely brick-veneer house with a rose garden and a formal entrance. There was a nice silver tea set on the table with tea and biscuits. What really made an impression – and what was most disarming – was that when John walked in he was wearing really, really ordinary work clothes. He took off his gumboots. I was quite struck by that. He was charming and kind. He told me, 'I'm so glad you're here. I hope that you will make the most of it.'

When I arrived at Melbourne Airport I was wearing a sari, because that's what I used to wear in India. I remember thinking, *I hope people aren't going to tell me I can't wear this anymore.* But the first thing the nuns at the school at which I taught said to me was, 'I hope you'll keep wearing it – it's such a beautiful dress.' Miniskirts were in vogue, and I suppose the nuns probably thought, *Well, we don't approve of miniskirts and the sari is much better*! When I later went to teach at the university in Ballarat, the director asked me if I always wore my 'national costume'. I replied, 'This is not a "national costume". These are my clothes!' He said, 'Well, it will be lovely to have some colour on the campus.'

I always wore the sari. Nowadays you hear all these terrible stories about women not being able to wear a headscarf, that it is working against them in terms of discrimination and stereo-types. I think to myself how lucky I was that no one felt that way about me. I wore the sari because that was what I was comfortable in. I experienced an amazing amount of tolerance. In fact, people liked it, and they were always asking me about it, or asking me to show them how to put one on. Some of the Australian women even borrowed my saris to wear for special occasions.

I was the only Indian person in Echuca. My Indian friends living in big Australian cities would say to me, 'Come to Melbourne. It's a one-horse town where you are, it must be terrible.' Then they came to visit and were amazed to see how hospitable it was and how many friends I had. You know what it's like in the big city. People can't be bothered. I had this unique experience living in country Australia. People were interested in me and my country, and they were interested in my culture. I wasn't left on the outside, I was very much a part of local society and welcomed by everyone I met.

If it hadn't been for my Echuca experience, I think I would have packed my bags and gone back to India. I certainly missed my family back in India too but I had left my own country for better opportunities: for my independence, and for the chance to explore my future. Australia gave me the freedom to live my life in a way I wanted and to choose my own path. I loved the Australian people. They were open and interested in me.

Ballarat today still has one of the highest percentages of Anglo-Celtic people in the country, so you can imagine what it was like when I arrived here. I was the first Indian person aside from a single student at the university. There was hardly anyone here from any other country. It was very white and yet I had a similar experience as I had in Echuca. I know from Ballarat, where I am involved with refugees, that country people always open their doors to help. They are more compassionate and go out of their way to do things for newcomers. One local woman took in an Iranian refugee, got him work and settled him in the community without being asked. When about six or eight students from West Papua came to Ballarat, we helped them all find a place to live.

Sometimes I find it hard to understand when people talk about prejudice. I know it's there, and I'm not denying it. But on a personal level? I've not experienced it. I've been extremely fortunate. I have felt a part of the community, always. Even now, with the coronavirus, people in my neighbourhood have been caring. I live on a small street, and when I came here, I was a young woman and everyone was old. I wasn't treated as an outsider. The neighbours left vegetables at my front door. Someone left eggs. Everyone was so friendly. They were so ready to accept someone who was different, who looked different, who dressed differently.

Now I am the second oldest person on my street and I have taken on the role of a community elder, so to speak. When I notice that there is a new baby, I take a little gift. The neighbours still look after me. When they go to the shops, they ask me if I need anything. It was recently my fifty-second Anzac Day in Australia, so I joined my neighbours in our driveways with candles, and I thought, *I'm a part of this too*. I said to myself, *I am an Australian, not just on paper, but because of all the feelings I have for this community*.

I understand that it is a scary time. It's something Australians who are alive today have not known before. One has to be resolute and understand that circumstances are not going to be as they are now forever and ever. We have to do our best to get on with our daily lives. We can accept that, at the moment, things aren't easy but then we need to ready ourselves to face events as they are. There will be different stages in the growth of every human being, and this is one of those instances where something externally imposed will challenge us all to cope.

There will inevitably be obstacles in life and, over the years, there have certainly been situations that required resilience from me. Those situations contributed to making my life different, interesting and worthwhile. I've always believed that thinking something is beyond me won't help me grow as a person. Coming to Australia has meant a lot of change, but by and large I've faced those changes with courage. I've dealt with them. I have the ability to reflect, to think deeply about a situation and to be ready for aspects that may be difficult. I remain ready. I do not give up. I do not say, 'No, this is too much for me.' I understand how things are, and then I figure out how I am going to cope.

Lakshmi Maksay died aged eighty-one, only weeks prior to the publication of Untold Resilience. *She lived in Ballarat and shared her story with Kristine Ziwica.*

'I want younger people to know that you do recover. Even the hard things that happen, like the trauma I've had in my life from losing loved ones, you still eventually come to terms with it. You never forget but you learn to cope, because you have to.'

Marie Wynn

I was sixteen, he was twenty and Leslie was the first person I ever fell in love with. It's difficult to try to describe the intensity of emotions in regard to relationships during that period. Those times were different from the casual sorts of relationships of following generations, especially today. We were so aware of the horrors of war. The daily war bulletins took over our lives. People say you can't fall in love when you're very young like that, but I did.

I lived in Wellington, New Zealand: a country at the bottom of the world that was in the process of making a slow, difficult recovery from the Great Depression. In 1939, World War II came. Though we were spared the everyday tragedy faced by others around the world, we did do it tough. Jobs were scarce and my parents, along with so many other folks, had a hard time trying to make ends meet. I am the eldest of four children.

My father suffered poor health and that made things hard for my mother. All his life, my father was in and out of hospital. I have a capacity to make the best of opportunities and not give up when the going gets tough. That comes from my upbringing and from my parents' situation.

Living through the Great Depression and having to get by with what we had has stayed with me. My kids laugh at me now because I still waste nothing. Back then it was a time of deprivation. Along with the blackouts, strict rationing was introduced. Meat and sugar were rationed and you couldn't buy sweets in the shops. We never had butter, either. As young girls, we were without male company. Our young men were all serving overseas and so us girls used to spend our free time dancing. All the girls had special shoes for dancing. Mine were silver. We had no pretty clothes or makeup. Silk stockings were unobtainable, so it was customary to paint your legs and draw a black line at the back to give the illusion of wearing stockings.

Our family wasn't very well-to-do but my parents did their best for me and my siblings and the community. I've always tried to emulate them. My mother was the one who moulded my life. She was a gentle person, but determined. She was kind but she was also strong because she had a lot to cope with, as my father was so unwell. I get a lot of my determination to push ahead from my mother. I go about this in a quiet way, like she did.

With the bombing of Pearl Harbor in 1941 and the entry of America into the war, everything changed for us. The threat of invasion by Japan was real and, even at my age, I was aware of the tension that hung over my country. American armed forces had been sent to the South Pacific to combat the Japanese. The fierce Battle of Guadalcanal took place in 1942, and the US Marine Corps divisions were sent to New Zealand for rest and recuperation prior to further military engagements and battle. My first contact with the Americans was in my own home. With all these young men returning, battle-weary, from the Solomon Islands, the citizens of Wellington were requested to open their homes and welcome them; to provide some home comforts as part of the war effort. My parents did what they could.

When the young American men were in town, there were also requests for young women to enrol at the various service clubs to entertain the troops. This we did *very* willingly, as we all loved to dance. My girlfriends and I lived for the opportunity to go to the dances. Since our young men were off serving, it was great to meet lads our own age. Times were different then. These clubs were strictly run, and no alcohol was permitted. We were carefully scrutinised before acceptance and told we had to behave like ladies. We dressed as well as we could, which was simply. This was the time immediately preceding rock and roll; a time of the jitterbug and the waltz and the foxtrot. I loved to dance and had been going out with one particular marine named Pat in 1943. But one night, everything changed.

It was a Sunday evening, and a friend and I went to the dance hall. Shortly after we arrived, a tall, handsome young marine asked me to dance. But as it turned out, he couldn't dance – he absolutely had two left feet! We spent the evening in each other's company and he eventually asked to take me home. His name was Leslie and that was the beginning of our story. There were no taxis available, so we caught the tram back to Strathmore Park where I lived. It was in the blackout, and as we were walking up the street – arm in arm, laughing together – I heard a voice saying, 'Is that you, Marie?' It was my father and he was accompanied by Pat. You see, Pat had been waiting at my house all evening, expecting me to be there. What a situation.

Pat and Leslie must have caught the tram home together. I don't know what the atmosphere was like. Pat contacted me at work the next day and I told him it was all off. It was a brief call, I might tell you. I wasn't cruel. I was never unkind like that but I made it clear that I was smitten with this other guy and of course I was sorry about it. Pat was a nice lad and he accepted it. This is what I mean when I say 'I was lucky' because the guys I met as a young girl were real gentlemen. Leslie was there from then on.

The 2nd Marine Division to which Leslie was attached was based at Camp Paekakariki, which was about an hour by train from Wellington. On the days he had liberty, I would find him waiting for me outside my building after work and we would either go home or entertain ourselves. My parents really took to Leslie and his friends – or 'buddies', as the Americans called them. In fact, my parents threw him a party for his twenty-first birthday. During that evening, one of Leslie's closest friends, Warren, had a severe attack of malaria and my mother took great care of him. It was a fun night. We didn't dance because Leslie wasn't much of a dancer but we both loved the big band music of Glenn Miller and Tommy Dorsey and Benny Goodman.

On my seventeenth birthday, Leslie gave me the first of many beautiful gifts: a lovely gold cross, which I still have and treasure today. He used to occasionally bring me sweets. And one time, he gave me a comb. In those days we only had access to wooden combs and you can imagine trying to comb your hair with one of those. It was impossible! Leslie was staggered at my amazement when he handed me an ordinary little plastic comb. I responded like he was giving me gold. Leslie couldn't get over my expression of joy when I saw it. He was the first person to ever send me flowers. They arrived at the office, a beautiful bunch of tulips. New Zealand boys didn't make those kinds of romantic gestures.

The arrival of Leslie's division in Wellington made such a huge impact on our lives. We had the company of young men, who were personable and charming. They were extremely well-mannered, these boys. Wherever you went they opened doors for you, they pulled out the chair for you to sit down, and they treated you with absolute respect. Of course, we had known the US marines would eventually be going into battle but we had no idea when and it was kept a secret. When it did happen, it was confirmed only on the morning of their departure. Leslie and I hadn't even spoken about it before it happened. We were enjoying the time and probably not thinking about what was ahead.

We had been gifted six glorious months together when our romance came to its sudden end. When all the ships in the harbour were being loaded my friends and I went to the top of the MLC building, where I worked. It was a sight I will never forget. We were standing on that big, tall building overlooking Wellington Harbour, watching the entire fleet leaving, without even a chance to say goodbye. I was really upset that night when I got home, and my mother, in trying to comfort me, said, 'You will never forget your first love.' She was right. I never did – and neither did he.

All of Leslie's letters came to me on military airmail letter-head with the words, 'Somewhere in the South Pacific with the Marines.' We were in regular communication. In the dreadful battles of Tarawa and Saipan many young men were killed and injured, including friends of Leslie. One of them was Warren Bedford who, on his twenty-first birthday, was killed right beside Leslie. The casualty lists in our newspapers were horrendous. Our devastation proved how the people of Wellington had taken these young men into their hearts and homes. Leslie was wounded in the Battle of Saipan, so he was shipped back to a naval hospital in Hawaii before being repatriated to the United States. He had been shot in the leg.

I would have only been eighteen when Leslie was sent back to the United States. He would have been about twenty-two. That was the end of the war for him and for a while we kept in touch. I sent him photos of what I was doing in New Zealand and he sent me photos and gifts. We wrote for about two years but eventually I started going out with other men and we sort of drifted apart. It was a gradual loss. I had such wonderful memories of Leslie but I knew it was time for me to move on. Eventually, I would wear my silver dancing shoes on my wedding day, when I married my husband Frank. I had a beautiful new dress for the occasion. I kept all those letters and photos from Leslie until I got engaged, and then I burned them. I gave a fine gold lavalier pendant he'd given me to my mother. She had it made into a brooch but then lost it.

I would have been in my fifties when Frank and I were on holiday in America with our friends, Marie and David. Over the course of the trip Marie kept saying, 'I know you've got this friend here. Why don't you give him a call?' And I said, 'No.' I knew Leslie owned bookstores in San Francisco. He'd sent me a letter about them at some stage. He had told me the name, so I had looked it up and knew the number to call. We were at the airport and our husbands were waiting for us in the departure lounge when Marie said, 'Oh, go on!' I had to put coins in the slot to make the call. I only had a few. I rang and it was *Leslie* who answered the phone! He immediately wanted to drive to the airport, but I wouldn't let him.

I never, ever told Frank. I didn't want him to think there was anything in it. And truly, there wasn't. I loved Frank dearly. It was just a matter of nostalgia and my coins were running out so I had to go. I was married to Frank for almost forty-four years. He passed away from a cerebral haemorrhage right before our anniversary. He was a fit man, and the last person you would expect to pass away so young. It was shocking for me. Devastating. I never thought I'd marry again because I wasn't interested in other men at all.

But then it happened. I met Brin, who was like a soothing balm to me. I married him in August 1996, five years after Frank passed away. Brin was such a comfort in those years after losing Frank, but then in 2002 he died as well. Brin had a severe stroke and was paralysed so he could no longer walk. I looked after him in his final year at home and thankfully we could still talk to each other.

But I always had this memory of Leslie. And, because of that, my two daughters knew about him. I was in Australia visiting my daughter, Jenny, and her family some years later and the topic came up. Jenny was telling my granddaughter, Amanda, about us when she suggested I get in touch with Leslie. I said, 'Heavens no. Not at this stage of my life! And who knows, he mightn't still be around, and if he is, he might be married, and if he is, there is no way I'm going to do anything about that. Don't be ridiculous!'

They all said, 'Oh, go on. You've got nothing to lose.'

I told them, 'No.'

One month after that, I was home in New Zealand and received an email from Amanda saying, 'Nanna, I've found a whole list of people in America and I think one of them might be the Leslie that you were talking about.' She referred to Leslie Richard Groshong, who lived in Oregon. I said, 'That won't be him. The man I knew lived in San Francisco, California.' I happened to be looking through some old correspondence some days later and thought, 'Oh, well, maybe I will write, and just find out if he's still around. There's no harm done.' I included my email address on the bottom of the letter, along with the words, 'If you're a relative or if you know him, I would be interested in making contact with this man who I knew all those years ago.'

A few days later I received an email. It said: 'It's me.'

From then on, we never missed a day.

Leslie had not forgotten me. He'd married, had two boys of his own and later divorced, but he'd kept every one of my photos. I'd destroyed all of his, but there you go. I flew out to America when I was eighty-one and he was eighty-five. I walked off the plane and, well, there he was. I remembered Leslie as this young, very good-looking man in uniform. You can imagine how attractive they looked back then. All those years later he was still a tall, fine-looking man who had aged, of course, but was still handsome. He really was. It was amazing. Here was this guy after all those years, and I didn't even hesitate. I walked straight up to him and he took me in his arms. I didn't cry and neither did he but he was obviously thrilled to be with me.

I went back to Leslie's house. There were flowers there for me, and he'd had a room made up so I would have my privacy. It didn't happen, though! I stayed there for a couple of months. It was just great. We picked up where we left off, and we never stopped because when I went home we still kept talking every day. It's true that we were both mature people by then. There was a difference, but it didn't *feel* different. I think that time together was as romantic as our younger years. When you get old, people probably think that you get past all those feelings, but you don't. If you love someone, it's as powerful and as strong as when you're young.

Leslie wanted to marry me, but even after all of that, I never would have married him. I couldn't lose a third husband. Six months after I came home, he flew to New Zealand to spend a month with me. I then flew back to America with him and had my first white Christmas. The night I flew back with him was the night that Barack Obama became president. Then after that trip he didn't come out again because of his health. I went back and forth another three times, the last of which was at the end of 2010. I was having some problems with my hips. Maybe from all the dancing when I was young. So I moved to Australia in 2011 to have my hips done and be closer to my daughter.

At the same time, Leslie went into care because he was having these terrible turns with diabetes. He became very ill. Initially, we still kept in touch by computer but it reached the stage where Leslie couldn't type anymore so, instead of emailing, we'd call each other every day. One day I rang and someone else answered. Leslie had been taken into hospital. Of course, I was really worried, so the next day I rang and they told me he had died. That was on 14 January 2015, and that was the end of our story.

I've had some terribly sad times in my life, especially with the loss of Frank, my first husband. However, with Leslie, along with the sadness, there was also a sense of closure. I had feelings of peace and thankfulness for the time we'd had together. After all, at this stage of our lives, it was a blessing that we'd had the remarkable opportunity to meet again. What more could we have wished for than to have that time? It couldn't go on forever at our age. So it was a peaceful grief, really, and my family was there for me.

My life has been blessed with love, and not just romantic love either. My daughters, Jennifer and Sharon, their husbands, Neville and Andrew, along with my five grandchildren and eight great-grandchildren, are my pride and joy. They give me support and comfort. Who could ask for more? As a young woman, I didn't want to miss out on anything. I tried to always look on the bright side, but it was difficult during the war years. It was the same for us then as it is for the young ones today, with this terrible virus. It's hard on them because at the time they want to be kicking up their heels and going out and enjoying themselves, they're held back.

I want younger people to know that you do recover. Even the hard things that happen, like the trauma I've had in my life from losing loved ones, you still eventually come to terms with it. You never forget but you learn to cope because you have to. If you don't learn this, you'll make yourself miserable. I'm sure my capacity to love stems from my parents, particularly my mother. I think I've always had a large capacity to love people, I really have, and I've been lucky that it's been reciprocated.

During one of our phone calls when he was in care, Leslie asked me to send him a copy of the last email he wrote. I printed it and posted it to him. It said:

Marie, I love your last email to me. You showed yourself to be the woman that I have loved and still love very much. We both realise that time has run out on the wonderful life that we had being physically together, but our love still shines through, bright and alive. Looking back over the many years that we have known each other and considering the beauty of our love I have no regrets for whatever happens next. Not even when. I love you dearly dear. Les.

We knew we weren't going to see each other again.

We knew that, but he just loved hearing from me. He really did.

Marie Wynn is ninety-four years old and lives in the Gippsland region of Victoria. Marie shared her story with Emily J. Brooks.

*'I learned to live, work and get along
with people with different ideas or
values from mine. To treasure family
and friends. To count my blessings. Not
to worry about material possessions.
My motto became: is it a question of
life and death?'*

Edith Sheldon

When I look back at my life, I can barely believe how lucky I was
to survive the horrors of the Holocaust and to have reached the
age of ninety-three. Even after the war, things were not easy, but
luck came my way again when I was offered a chance of a new
life in distant Australia. I was also lucky to have met and married
Walter, my soulmate for sixty years. And I am lucky to have two
sons and four grandsons I can be proud of. I teach them to appreciate what they have and most of all to not do harm to others.

When hard times come, you have to face them. Most of my
friends lost their parents in Auschwitz or one of the camps.
They actually watched them die. My hardships pale beside their
unfathomable losses. I don't see myself as especially resilient.
Resilience isn't a cloak you can pull on to guard against tough
times. When I was in the concentration camp, with the fear of
being transported hanging over my head every day, it simply

became part of life. I simply tried to survive. The only things that helped me were my sturdy disposition and positive outlook.

I was born in Prague, Czechoslovakia, in 1927. My father, Otto Drucker, studied civil engineering at the German University in Prague and then, during World War I, served as an officer in the Austro-Hungarian army. He and my mother, Ida Auerbach, had met before the war. They fell in love instantly and became devoted sweethearts. After the war, on 28 October 1918, Czechoslovakia was proclaimed a republic. The new nation embraced Bohemia, Moravia, Slovakia, Sub-Carpathia and a small part of Silesia. It was an exciting, enlightened time. The old empire was gone, modern ideas filled the schools and universities; intellectual optimism took off.

My father resumed his studies, graduated, and tried to find work. In those days, you wouldn't marry unless you had a steady job to support your wife and family. When that finally happened, my parents wed in December 1924. They'd been engaged for nearly ten years and sadly had just four years of happy married life ahead of them. When I was two years old, my father died of a middle ear infection. I have no memory of him, though I did feel his loss deeply because of the impact it had on my mother. She was overcome by grief; she wore her widow's weeds – black clothes and a heavy black veil – way beyond the customary year of mourning. She visited my father's grave every week, wailing and crying. I went with her and then eventually stopped her from going. Even though I was a small child, I knew that this was damaging her. She never remarried, or even had a male friend.

After my father's death, Mum had a small pension, but it wasn't enough for us to live on. So, Mum went back to work to support us. Before her marriage, she had worked as a music teacher at a finishing school for well-to-do young ladies. After my father's death, she took up teaching the piano again, and later she also taught German. Grandmother Louise, Mum's mother, moved in with us to help out and we became very close. Our home was a flat in a nice, newly built block in a solid, if unfashionable, middle-class part of Prague. The flat was typical for our district, with two larger rooms, two small rooms plus a kitchen, bathroom, toilet and larder. There was a cellar to store coal, wood and potatoes for the winter but no running hot water, central heating or lifts. We also had no radio or telephone and, of course, no car. When the Nazis invaded, not having a radio meant we did not know what was happening.

The Depression was awful, with mass unemployment, poverty and food queues. Mum had had a poor childhood, so she knew what it felt like to have nothing. She was extremely generous by nature and during the Depression years she kept a big pot of soup on the stove and would give soup and a slice of bread to the beggars who knocked on our door. On the hill beyond my school was a colony of old railway carriages where a large number of destitute people lived. Their only water came from a pump on the street, which would freeze up in winter. Their children came to our school in rags. So Mum asked me to bring two children home for lunch each Tuesday and Thursday. When I objected that they were dirty and smelly, Mum said, 'If you could not wash, you would be the same.'

Today's younger generations wouldn't understand how we lived; they have grown up in times of plenty. Even though we were relatively well-off, we still had to be careful with money and nothing was wasted. People would pull apart old hand-knitted sweaters, wash and stretch the wool and knit new garments. They would take their pants and coats to a tailor to turn them inside out to hide the sheen of years of wear. Being Jewish didn't mean a great deal to me. We were members of the Jewish community but didn't observe many religious practices and I didn't have Jewish friends. I loved learning; I went to a secular state school and studied hard. I was one of twelve to win a place at the new local selective high school. I attended for two years, but then Jewish children were banned from schools and I was devastated.

After Hitler came to power in Germany in 1933, news of the persecution of Jews filtered through to us. Mum became very apprehensive about our future. On the night of the Munich crisis we were expecting a German invasion. We sat and waited in Grandma's room, which Mum thought was safest from potential gas attacks, as it had no external window. Czechoslovakia's English and French allies betrayed us, accepting Hitler's demands. British Prime Minister, Neville Chamberlain, declared 'peace for our time' in his 30 September 1938 address, after handing over the Sudetenland border areas of our country to Germany. My mother fully understood what was happening to Jews in Austria and Germany, and knew immediately that it was the end of our way of life. From that moment, our world was filled with fear.

On 15 March 1939, Hitler and his army invaded Prague and the remaining parts of the republic. That was the end of my childhood. I was twelve years old. In the coming days, Jewish assets were confiscated and bank accounts frozen. We had to hand in any jewellery, shares, insurance policies and portable musical instruments. We were not allowed to go to parks, sit on public benches or use public transport. We had an 8 pm curfew and could only shop after 3.30 pm, by which time most goods had disappeared. We were barred from having professions, going to entertainment venues and from mixing with non-Jews. The Nazis went from house to house making enquiries: Any Jews living here? This was when I started to feel really scared. Non-Jews responded in different ways: some did not want to know us anymore while others tried to help us, even at their own peril.

Soon, Jews were thrown out of their homes. We were fortunate that, though we had to vacate our flat to make way for a Nazi family, we were given a similar but smaller flat across the road. We were barred from school, but the Jewish community didn't give up and organised alternative opportunities for us. Older students and professionals taught us the normal school curriculum in 'circles' of six children of the same age. We had to constantly change venues – meeting in different homes, arriving separately so as not to draw the neighbours' attention – but we did manage to sit the end-of-year exams. I felt deprived, but the future never entered my mind because it was all about getting through each day. I would advise students missing out on their studies during this current pandemic to concentrate on the things they love. Be prepared to adapt to the new situation.

Then in November 1941, the unthinkable happened. The 'transports' began, and Jews in Prague were systematically rounded up. The German occupation regime forced the Jewish community to organise this process. Someone would come at night with a piece of paper saying you had to present yourself at the Trade Fair pavilion two or three days later with your transport number around your neck. Our family had two suitcases permanently packed in preparation. The rule was up to 50 kg per person. This included a suitcase, a rucksack and a bedding roll. In addition, we could pack a bag with food for three weeks.

They took Grandmother Louise first. I cannot bear thinking about it, especially now that I am old myself. She was over eighty by then. We felt so helpless when they threw her onto a lorry to take her away. It was dreadful. We had no idea what would happen to her. A month later, it was our turn. Mum and I were transported together and our numbers were AAw 461 and 462. We had been told that the SS randomly weighed luggage on arrival at the Trade Fair and if it was even slightly overweight they would confiscate that family's entire luggage. The next morning, Mum borrowed a large set of scales from the grocery downstairs, and then had to decide what to take and what to put in the rucksack or the suitcase.

I am sad to say that many neighbours kept ringing our doorbell when it became known we were 'in a transport'. 'Surely you will not leave this, or that, to the Germans?' they would ask, of the items we were leaving behind. Mum called them vultures, and it made her sad to see the greed of former friends. In truth, we could not hand over anything even if we had wanted to. We had already made a list of all our possessions and handed that list to the Germans. In our dining room there were chairs with beautiful embroidered seats. The funny thing was, my mother had always put covers on them, so I had no idea the seats were so lovely. As soon as we knew we were being transported she took the covers off, saying we might as well enjoy them. It was treasured furniture like this that the neighbours wanted to claim for themselves.

When we left, the worst part was locking our front door behind us. It really was the end of our life as we knew it, and the uncertainty about the future was terrifying. On arrival at the Trade Fair we had to hand in any money, our keys, papers, the inventory of our flat and anything of value. For Mum, the reality of leaving her treasured possessions behind impacted her sense of self. These were items she had worked so hard to own; they represented her domain, her identity. It was the start of a process of dehumanisation that the Nazis used, stripping us of everything. We spent three days at the Trade Fair under constant SS harassment. There were no toilets, just latrines. There was nowhere to wash, and food was scarce. The dirty floor was divided into strips numbered one to 1200. You had to sit and sleep on your numbered square and stand up when an SS came by.

Before daybreak on 3 August 1942, the guards marched us to a little railway station in nearby Bubny. The train was grossly overcrowded. People stood, or sat on luggage racks or on the floor – wherever they could. The train finally left and my relief was great when I saw the familiar landmarks – we were going to Theresienstadt. We knew Theresienstadt well because both sides of my family had lived there when it was a garrison town and we had often visited them before the war. Now it was different. The small town had been transformed into a Ghetto, a transit camp to 'concentrate' Jews before their transport to death camps in the east. By August 1942, the little fortress town of Theresienstadt, which had once housed just 7000 soldiers and civilians, held over 53,000 people.

We arrived at about midday at Bohusovice station and were made to form a column and walk, carrying our luggage, 4 km to the Ghetto. We were under escort of gendarmes with their bayonets drawn. The weather was boiling hot, and we all wore several layers of clothing, so as to have more clothing available for winter. I had on a summer frock, then a blouse and a heavy grey skirt (into the hem of which I had secretly sewn some banknotes), a cardigan, a jacket, and a light coat, and three pairs of panties and stockings. Upon arrival at the Ghetto, a man suddenly darted across the road and grabbed Mum's 'Fress-Tasche' – a large bag with her food in it. The man was Mr Steindler, an old friend of the family. At that moment, I was truly shocked that he would steal our food. What I didn't realise was that he actually took a great risk for us.

We trudged on, bewildered, tired and thirsty, into a barracks called the Schleusse. We had to file past several SS and Czech gendarmes seated behind a long table. This was the place where new prisoners were assessed and their fates decided. We had to put our luggage on the table to be searched, and they stole whatever took their fancy. Luckily, a Czech gendarme secretly motioned to me to put my 'Fress-Tasche' on the floor, and push it along with my foot; thus, all the food I carried was saved. Later that day, Mr Steindler reappeared with Mum's bag, and we learned later that the SS had confiscated all the suitcases belonging to the whole transport.

Eventually, we were allowed to leave the barracks and made our way to lodgings near the town square. There, we were allocated floor space in a shop already full of women. The premium spots along the walls were already taken, so we had to sleep in the middle or near a door, where everyone stepped on us during their frequent trips to the latrines at night. Diarrhoea was rampant. Meanwhile, I found out that Grandmother Louise was still alive. I went to look for her, while Mum guarded our floor spaces and the remains of our luggage. Grandma, bless her soul, had saved most of the food we had given her a month earlier, and she wanted us to have it.

The next day a relation called Mr Taussig found us and gave us some good advice as to how to avoid the dreaded transports to Poland. He said that Mum should apply for work as a *Siechenschwester,* a nurse for old people. It was a job no one wanted to do as it meant working six twelve-hour day or night shifts. The work involved carrying cold water in buckets up several stories to the wards several times per day. There were very few sanitation aids and the pervasive smell was horrific, as the poor old people were unable to digest the almost inedible food. Mum was exhausted and contracted a bad hernia from all the heavy lifting. But it was a 'protected' job at that time. I only realised when I had children myself why she endured it. She had to stay alive for me. At the end of the war, Mum looked seventy years old even though she was only forty-eight.

When I told Mr Taussig that I had learned drawing and painting, he suggested I apply for a job in the painting atelier. The SS had established it to make themselves extra money and this too was a protected job. When I went to apply for the job, I mounted the steps to the second floor of the Nazi headquarters with shaking knees. I was really scared. Thankfully I got the job, and the person who employed me was the head of the studio, and not a German.

The job required colouring in bookmarks and little pictures which the SS then sold. If you could not finish 100 pictures per day, or were not good enough, you lost your job and your protection. It was very stressful, fifty-four hours work per week, but I managed. At times I lifted my head for a second to look at the nearby hills, wishing I were a bird.

We soon realised that transports to the east were leaving Theresienstadt every three days. We thought they were deporting Ghetto inmates to some godforsaken labour camp in Poland. We didn't know about the extermination camps or about Auschwitz.

I was moved to the so-called 'Girls' Home' and I was happy to escape the cramped conditions in the shop. Each floor housed around 200 girls who shared just two toilets. There was a large military style washroom on the ground floor, with cold water only, which we all used. Soap was in short supply, as were paper and toiletries. For a while, we used prayer-book pages to clean ourselves, but even those ran out. Fortunately, our periods had stopped after our arrival. We thought that they must have put something in the soup because it happened to all of us but looking back, I think it was stress. I was gradually getting weaker and came down with a bad case of chickenpox, then infectious jaundice.

My grandma died a miserable death on 25 March 1943, having contracted pneumonia after a delousing procedure. At the time, I didn't know she had died. I was sick in the hospital, and I had no idea what was happening because Mum couldn't talk to me as she was also ill in a different hospital. When I got out, I learned what had happened to Grandma. They chased her outdoors in winter for delousing and they shaved her head. It was horrible. However, I was also relieved she had died and was therefore spared from being sent to Poland. All my life I have felt bad about not having been able to help my grandma during her last days.

At the start of 1943, typhoid spread through the Ghetto. When I developed a high fever and diarrhoea, I realised I was infected. I still remember Dr Stern injecting me, perhaps to strengthen my heart. By then, I was extremely weak. I could not stand or walk and was emaciated. Dr Stern told Mum to say her goodbyes to me as I would not last till the morning. I was eventually taken to one of the children's typhoid hospitals on a stretcher. Mum thought she had lost me. I was delirious most of the time. Dr Stern was a good man and he certainly saved my life. I was finally discharged in August 1943 but by then, my meagre possessions had disappeared as it was rumoured that I had died.

Our lives there were ruled by two things: constant hunger and fear of being transported to Poland. But we were lucky. Incredibly, there were also moments of sheer joy in the camp. Friendships and little things like getting extra morsels to eat, a flower blooming in the grass or a warm ray of sunshine in winter were all amplified. It was in music that the real magic happened. The Germans had imprisoned a great number of outstanding artists, writers and scientists in the Ghetto. Many of them tried to improve the lives of their fellow inmates by organising choirs, giving recitals or lectures. There were many wonderful concerts given; a children's opera, *Brundibár*, was performed, and also Verdi's 'Requiem'. I lived in that music and forgot where I was when I read it. I can still sing the operas, and the 'Requiem' I can hear in my head from beginning to end. It lifts me to a special place.

When rumour spread, in May 1945, that the Russians were coming, we all ran onto the dark street, excited and jubilant. At first, I was euphoric, but it soon wore away. When the Red Army liberated Theresienstadt, many survivors were desperately ill and died soon after. Tragedy was everywhere. My years in Theresienstadt Ghetto influenced my life, my outlook, my attitudes and my moral compass. I learned to live, work and get along with people with different ideas or values from mine. To treasure family and friends. To count my blessings. Not to worry about material possessions. My motto became: is it a question of life and death? When the COVID-19 pandemic hit, I was of course considered vulnerable. But it hasn't made me anxious. I will have to go sooner or later.

Edith Sheldon is ninety-three years old and lives in Sydney. Edith shared her story with Juliet Rieden.

'How could we have been so thoughtless not to consider the dead as well as the living? What a lot we had to learn. Without even trying, Fatima taught me about love, strength, suffering and the importance of human dignity.'

Phoebe Wynn-Pope

I have learned, through my life and particularly as an aid worker, that practicality is an essential tool. The world presents challenges, from disasters to war, on both a grand and complex scale. Many of them are playing out today as we continue to count the losses and suffering caused by the COVID-19 pandemic. Anger and outrage in the face of this disastrous situation can be necessary and are probably warranted. But for me, what helps most is being able to say, 'This is what I am confronted with right now. This is how I am going to deal with it today.'

It is dealing with what is happening today that has made it possible for me to continue, when I have borne witness to immense suffering and hardship. What is the alternative when those experiencing the suffering and hardship do just that themselves? I have seen extraordinary acts of resilience, many demonstrated by women living in war and disaster zones.

I learned an awful lot from their determination to survive – and thrive – in unimaginably challenging circumstances.

I grew up in rural Victoria and many of the people I knew were members of the Australian Red Cross. My mother has been a member for more than sixty years, and Red Cross volunteers were always on the farm when we had bull sales or a fete. Sandwiches, it was always loaves and loaves of sandwiches, and scones. The wonderful Red Cross ladies would arrive with their smiles and supplies, seemingly effortlessly providing sustenance for hundreds of people at a time. When I was very small, a dear friend and I baked some cakes and held a stall for the Red Cross outside the shearers' quarters. The jackaroos and station hands all dutifully came and bought a cupcake or two and we raised $7.20. We were so proud of ourselves.

My father, Malcolm Fraser, was in politics and he would go on to become the Australian prime minister. It may be contrary to the popular view of politicians, but he spent his life trying to bring about change for the better. Between my mother and father, I always understood that we were lucky, and that we should try to make a contribution. We rarely travelled as a family – school holidays were spent on the farm. But I was drawn to the idea of people living in different parts of the world with different ways of life. For some reason, Africa fascinated me, and I always wanted to travel there. I was captivated by how little I knew about the people, the wildlife and the countryside and was keen to learn more.

CARE Australia was a relatively new organisation in Australia at the time. In the 1980s, being an aid worker was an unusual occupation. There were no degrees or professional training courses like there are now. I joined CARE Australia's Victorian office in 1989 as a fundraiser with the hope of working in Africa at some time. My first overseas trip with CARE was to Bangladesh, where I visited several projects including a women's micro-credit project designed to help lift women and their families out of poverty. As part of those projects, revolving loan funds were established and women participating received small 'micro-loans'. Access to credit allowed women to buy seeds or some chickens as a form of capital to break the cycle of debt.

The loans system helped address poverty, and there were associated benefits like better health, nutrition and education. I was lucky to be invited into those women's homes. They were immaculately cared for, tiny mud-floored houses, and I was able to talk with them about their new businesses and the hopes and dreams they had for their children and families. They taught me that the material things we take for granted can be a distraction from what's important. The homes they created were an expression of care and love. A mother's dreams for her children – to be healthy, safe and educated – are universal.

After working in the Melbourne office for a year, I realised that, despite my trip to Bangladesh, I still didn't understand enough about CARE's work to promote it convincingly to potential donors. I asked to work in the field for a short time. I wanted to learn more about our work and how it brought about positive change in people's lives, but I also knew there was so much to learn about other cultures and ways of life. It would be over six years before I returned to Australia. Over the coming years I worked in Thailand, Cambodia, Vietnam and Laos. As my knowledge base grew, my role expanded and scaled up too.

As CARE Australia's Emergency Response Manager, I was fortunate enough to work in Iran and then Iraq after the first

Gulf War. The suppression of the internal uprising in Iraq led to hundreds of thousands of Kurdish refugees crossing the border into neighbouring Iran. I led CARE's operations in Iran, and we provided food and water to over 400,000 people until they returned to their homes in Iraq. In Iraq, our school lunches program provided some normality for a population of people who were both tired and traumatised from the war. But this experience could not have prepared me for what was to come.

By 1992, I had finally made it to Africa, a place I had always been interested in and in which I wanted to work. I was based in Kenya when news of the famine in Somalia began to leak out of the country. This was before mobile phones were common, when we still relied on newspapers, faxes and a handful of television channels, and – if you were lucky – a satellite telephone the size of a kitchen table. CARE had a big operation in Mogadishu that was largely run out of the Kenya office and we were all concerned about news from the south.

Our national director asked me to accompany him to assess the situation. It was shocking. The civil war in Somalia had only recently ended and the government had completely broken down. The country was being run by warlords who were heavily armed. Everyone had guns. It was a highly insecure environment, and that political insecurity coincided with one of the worst African droughts of the century. I saw markets that were completely empty, and famine had taken hold. Aid agencies were scrambling to provide the necessary assistance and it was a chaotic, difficult operating environment.

In the early days, we lived on pasta and tomato paste cooked over a coal fire until we could arrange for more consistent supplies. When we hired a car, it came with a driver and two gunmen. We understood that those gunmen were there to protect the car, not us. In today's humanitarian operating environment this would be considered completely unacceptable. Thousands of people had been displaced and were living in makeshift shelters in crowded camps, but I remember finding it oddly quiet. In truth, there was too much suffering for anyone to be making much noise. Kids sat around with flies crawling over their faces because they were simply too weak to brush them away. They were weak, sick, starving and it was completely shattering to witness. More than 100,000 people are thought to have died.

One day, we were wandering through one of the camps and I met a woman named Fatima whose face I can still see clearly today. She told me that she needed white cloth, which was unusual because most people requested water, food or shelter. I asked what it was for and she explained that she'd lost two of her children. Traditionally, Somalis wrap their dead in white cloth for burial. Fatima said if her children hadn't been able to live with dignity, she at least wanted them to be able to die with dignity. Meeting Fatima and hearing her request for white cloth to bury her dead children was a life-defining moment for me. I was stunned, shocked and devastated in turn. How could we have been so thoughtless not to consider the dead as well as the living? What a lot we had to learn. Fatima taught me about love, strength, suffering and the importance of human dignity.

Living back at home in Australia, after my field-work days were over, I often heard the suffering in poorer countries deprecated. People seem to think that grief and starvation are things you get used to. I have even heard people in developed nations say things like 'They are used to it' or 'They expect to lose some of their children, so it makes it easier'. This is a complete fallacy. To assume that someone's suffering is somehow different, that their pain is less severe because of its relentlessness, demeans the universality of the human condition. There is no loving mother or father who loses their child without an inexpressible heartache. I'm sure that my work overseas did shape my own parenting later on. Indeed, I suspect that the values that have guided me and my family are the values that compelled me to work overseas in the first place.

After spending the next couple of years based in the Middle East, I would return to Africa at the end of the Rwandan genocide. More than 800,000 people had been killed in the 100 days preceding my arrival in the neighbouring nation, the Democratic Republic of Congo (formerly Zaire). The worst of the war was over when I arrived, but the crisis was far from over. Rwandan refugees numbering 1.2 million had fled across the border. Normally home to 100,000 people, Goma was ridiculously crowded and the influx of refugees had put huge pressure on local resources. The scale of the crisis was absolutely enormous. Those that didn't live there were being encouraged to move north to Rutshuru, where several sites had been identified by UNHCR for refugee camps. There were two active volcanoes in the area. Thank God they didn't erupt; there would have been no escape.

My role was to undertake a needs assessment and establish CARE Australia's program there. Coordinating with other agencies, including the UN and Oxfam, who were responsible for water and sanitation, and with our colleagues from CARE Canada, we took on the work of camp management, food distribution and the provision of medical assistance. We also opened an Unaccompanied Children's Centre within the camp for the many lost or orphaned children who were on their own and needed specific care. The centre was full of both love and total devastation.

One day a man brought two tiny babies into the centre. Their mothers – his sister and his wife – had both given birth on the road, and subsequently died of cholera. We were the only hope those babies had, as he had no way of feeding them. His decision to leave the babies with us was devastating and I saw him weeping as he walked away. Our days were filled with such sorrow and, in a strange way, joy. I saw those abandoned babies given strength and a chance at life as they were coddled and loved by the ladies we had working with us.

The deaths of those babies' mothers was a harbinger of the cholera epidemic that was to come. Over three weeks, 70,000 people died. As we drove from Goma to the camps, I saw that men, women and children had wrapped their loved ones in their sleeping mats and left them carefully on the side of the road. There was no other option for them but to leave their loved ones behind and carry on. We called it the road of death. It made me so angry. They were senseless, pointless deaths that should have been prevented. As aid workers, we were all struggling with the extent of the suffering and the enormity of the task ahead. Some of the team were so desperately affected that they were medevaced out for psychological reasons while the rest of us carried on as best we could.

Rwanda today, though not without its challenges, is a country often held up as a model for economic development. It notably has the highest number of women in politics anywhere in the world and is a remarkable example of how communities and societies can go through the most horrendous experiences and still survive. I think it often comes down to resilience. There are many lessons to be learned from the strength and commitment of the Rwandan people and how determined they are to address the wrongs of the past and build a new future together. Fostering resilience is essential to surviving shocks and hardships. One of the things I loved about working with CARE in the field is that we worked with people, especially with women and girls, to identify vulnerabilities, strengthen capacity and infrastructure, and to build buoyancy into their daily lives. That resilience was able to help them minimise shocks and the inevitable hardships that would come in the future.

Our contributions as aid workers in these circumstances ranged from providing technical help, to limiting the impacts of increased flooding brought about by seasonal cyclones, to developing alternative income streams for farmers vulnerable to drought. The women I met and worked with in Rwanda, Somalia and so many other places, for whom daily survival was a challenge, taught me that real resilience comes from within.

After returning home to Australia, I wanted to learn about how to stop crises happening in the first place. I wanted to find out how to build a world with more stability, where people could grow, excel and live in peace. I thought if I could work in policy or strategy to help prevent the kinds of things that I'd seen then I could contribute more in the long term than being on the ground. I continued my work with CARE Australia while I did my master's, and during that time I had my boys, Harry and Hamish, who are now twenty-four and nineteen. I have been delighted to see them grow into kind, generous and compassionate young men. I received my PhD in

International Law in 2008, which focused on the role of the international community when confronting war crimes, crimes against humanity, and genocide. Rwanda was my case study. I wanted to prevent the kinds of things I'd seen on the ground from ever happening again.

Each time I came home from the field, the stark contrast between where I was compared to where I'd just been was visceral. I remember upon returning to Australia from Somalia, I'd just had lunch and a friend was throwing the scraps in the bin. There wasn't much food on the plate, but I had come from seeing children picking single seeds to eat out of the dirt. Throwing away any food seemed wrong. The feeling of material good fortune dulls over time and everything becomes normal again, but it can really slap you in the face.

It's this sense of proportion and disproportion that makes me think of a scene from the 2008 war movie *The Hurt Locker*. The main character, James, has just returned home to the United States after serving in the Iraq war. He's at the supermarket with his family when his wife asks him to grab a box of cereal and meet her at the checkout. When he gets to the cereal aisle, he just stares at the rows and rows of varieties, overwhelmed by the abundance and choice. I have felt like that quite often.

I am now Head of Business and Human Rights and Pro Bono at a Melbourne law firm; a role that has two key areas of work. The first is working with businesses to help them uncover and prevent human rights violations such as modern slavery in their operations and supply chains. The second is to run the firm's pro bono program. The driving force that has kept me doing what I do is the simple notion that a small contribution can make a massive difference in somebody's life.

In the 1990s I was drawn to the idea that a globalised world was going to be good for everybody. The Cold War had ended and there was a very real sense that what's good for the world would be good for us. That if we could lift people in Africa or Asia out of poverty, it would be good for the world. Over the last decade or so, with the rise of nationalism and increased fear, we've lost the type of leadership that promotes that idea.

By contrast, COVID-19 has shown us how interconnected we are, and we need serious global leadership and a return to that sense of common humanity to ensure that we don't regress. Strangely enough, life during the pandemic has been relatively normal for my family and me. I have been working from home which, having spent many years as a consultant, is not a new experience. I live in the country and we are lucky to have some space around us. I feel deeply for those who are living alone. Ultimately, we all love the same and cry the same. We just have different challenges – and some are more preventable than others.

Phoebe Wynn-Pope is fifty-four years old and lives on the Mornington Peninsula. Phoebe shared her story with Jamila Rizvi and Emily Joyce.

'My experiences as a young person help me get through this coronavirus pandemic. I am reminded, a little bit, of how it used to be during the war. The shops are all closed, like they were back then. It feels strangely similar in some ways.'

Lilia Graovac

I didn't have one cent in my pocket when I arrived in Australia as a young woman. Not a word of English either. Still, I wasn't scared because it was exciting. I was optimistic for the future and I had my brother with me on the journey over. I also knew that we were going to be reunited with my older brother soon, which was a huge comfort. He had a house where we could stay, in Ballarat in Victoria. Australians would speak to us in English, which I didn't understand at all at first. I could only speak Serbo-Croatian. It was different from what we were used to but thankfully there were a lot of migrants there in those days, and some of them Yugoslavian too. I sought out people from my part of the world and made friends that way. They're friends I still have today. We were all away from home, but we were together.

Not being able to speak English was difficult. I remember wanting to buy an ice cream. I went to the corner shop and couldn't communicate what I wanted. I ended up leaving without making a purchase. Then, on my way back home, I saw a piece of paper in the gutter with a picture of an ice cream on it. I squealed, picked it up and ran back to the shop, waving it to the man behind the counter. I got my ice cream: vanilla in a cone. I have always liked to learn, however it was possible, especially from others who could correct mistakes. Some people don't like to admit that they don't know, but I believe that you can always learn something from another person. I was lucky to learn English eventually but also fortunate to keep speaking my own language with my family. That gave me a connection to home.

My first job in Australia was in nursing. I worked at the St John of God hospital. It was one of the hardest things I've ever had to do in my life, working there without a word of English. When one of the patients wanted something, we wouldn't be able to understand one another. I couldn't tell the difference between some words, like 'pen' with which to write and 'pan' for the toilet. It was only if patients spoke to me slowly that I could comprehend what they were saying. Later, I worked at a nursing home and my English improved enormously. The old people liked me. They approved of how I arranged the pillows. They were always requesting me. I made friends with some of the other nurses there too and I've kept in touch with them. I was not lonely, nor was I sad or scared. I was many miles from my family, that's true, and I struggled with the language barrier. But other than that, I was pretty happy.

If my mother were alive today, I would tell her that she was a bit too strict on us girls. I wasn't allowed to go out as much as my brothers. They could stay out longer after the sun went down. When we came to Australia that was one of the imme-diate differences with home. Women my age were freer. They could come and go from home when they wished. Although now, life has changed for women all over the world. When I first lived in Australia, women wouldn't go to the pubs; they were more family-oriented and stayed at home with their children. Now it's different and, really, women can do anything.

I come from the city Zadar in what is now called Croatia. It was still Yugoslavia when we left. I was born in 1938, just before World War II began. I was one of six siblings: three girls and three boys. I'm the fourth in line. My childhood was poor, so my main memory of that time is hunger. I was always hungry. My childhood tastes like polenta. We basically lived on it; we had so much of the stuff. Breakfast, lunch and dinner: polenta, polenta, polenta. That's how we survived.

We had no pencils and books at primary school. We memo-rised whatever the teacher wrote on the blackboard. I learned the Serbian Cyrillic alphabet. I learned Latin and I spoke Croatian. I left school when I was thirteen years old, still a girl. It was in 1956, when I was on the verge of womanhood, that we left Yugoslavia. The situation in my country at the time wasn't rosy and my father never liked communism. We were happy to leave. My family decided it was safest to go to Italy. All of us went except one brother – my eldest brother, Neriko – who had escaped Yugoslavia and immigrated to Australia earlier. His life there was good.

The rest of the family was in Italy for two years before, ulti-mately, my other brother Bepino and I decided we wanted to go to Australia. I wanted what Neriko had: an Australian life. I also wanted to be with him. I was excited for the adventure.

It was a thrill even thinking of travelling that far. But we also had to leave everything behind, including the rest of our relatives. My cousins and I grew up together and so when we left I missed them the most. Bepino and I left Italy and the rest of our family by ship when I was twenty years old. The journey took thirty-five days and I slept in a room on board with eight other girls. It was not very comfortable. After ten days at sea I got horribly seasick. I was throwing up every day and couldn't leave my room.

When we first got to Australia, I lived with my two brothers and a widower with three young children, as well as another man, his wife and their son. We had one bathroom, which meant one toilet, between us. I had my own room, which was a luxury. Five years later, my other brother Alfio would come to join us too. I was like a mother to my three brothers. I did the laundry and the cooking. I didn't exactly enjoy it but I saw it as my duty. We were away from our parents and they needed to be cared for. My sister, Jolanda, remained in Italy with my parents. She married an Italian man and stayed there.

I thought of my family all the time. We didn't have a telephone then, so it was all about letters. I wrote to my sisters and my parents every week and sent money regularly. I would tell them about my job, about my life, about Australia. I felt close to them, even though they were far away. Even today, I still feel close to the ones who are alive. I talk to my sister every week on Skype. She has visited Australia three times. I learned long ago that you don't have to be physically close to your family in order to love them.

Coming to a new country is not so hard physically, but it is mentally. In the end, though, you have your own family, you make a new home, you get used to it and life goes on. Being surrounded by family, especially having my brothers with me when I first arrived, has helped me a lot. I also found love here, in Australia. I met my husband, Jovan, a few months after I arrived. Rather conveniently, he lived next door to us. He boarded with a German family. The first time I saw Jovan was when he was playing soccer with other migrants. I remember thinking he was cute. I knew even then that he was Serbian. But we were in love.

Our ethnicities weren't as big a problem as you might think they would have been. When I was growing up, we never had any tension between Serbians and Croatians. The two cultures weren't divided where we came from. I had always known Serbians and we had Serbian friends, even back in Yugoslavia. I never really heard much about tension with Serbia, though I did know they had a different religion to us. It was only when we lived in Australia that we learned about hatred between Croats and Serbs. I will never truly understand it. Even though I married someone from a different religion, my family was excellent. All my siblings and relatives accepted Jovan and now my brothers are his brothers too.

I was twenty and Jovan was twenty-five when we met. He was handsome, he had work, and he was able to provide for me and the family we would have. I remember when Jovan asked me to go out with him, one of my brothers was mad. He didn't want me going out with anyone and felt protective, particularly because our father wasn't around to play that role. Jovan and I went down the street on our first date and we didn't hold hands. I liked him immediately. It was not really the fashion at that time to go out to dinner, like couples might these days. It was more about going to the pictures or to dances. Pubs were only for men, so we couldn't go there either.

Every week there was a different dance on. There were Aussies and Italians, there were Polish people and Germans – and Croatians and Serbians. Jovan knew how to dance. It was one of the things I liked most about him. I didn't have many dresses with me, so I made some for myself. I'd go to the shop in Ballarat and see which dresses I liked, buy the material and the pattern and go home and sew one for myself. I'd wear a different dress every time but my favourite colour to wear was red. I loved being dressed in red.

Jovan and I got married after four years of dating. It wasn't considered right to live alone with your boyfriend, so he moved into the room with my brothers. Jovan helped a lot around the house. Not so much cleaning, but at least he cooked. He would help with the shopping too. Our engagement was not particularly romantic. It was more practical than anything. He just said to me one day 'I'm going to buy you a ring' and then he did. He didn't have any family at our wedding, which was sad. He tragically no longer had his parents. Our wedding was gorgeous, even though many of our family members could not be there. We were surrounded by friends.

Jovan's childhood had been difficult. He was in a concentration camp in Hungary for three years when he was just ten years old. In 1990, we would go back to find that concentration camp. We walked and walked until Jovan recognised the curve of a particular bridge. He used to tell me that growing up, he was hungry and scared for so long. The Red Cross took him from that camp and brought him to Yugoslavia, where Jovan was placed with foster parents. He and his sister were both forced to leave their parents. They were almost split up too but right before they left, their mother told them to hold hands and stay together, no matter what. It worked.

We'd both known hardship by the time we got together, but I was always aware of the additional sadness in his past. We made our own family here in Australia. We had a boy called Steven in 1963 and three years later, we had a daughter called Vivian. I was happy to have kids. I had always wanted to be a mother and we would have had more children, but could only really afford two. Jovan and I never had material worth. We didn't have a lot of money, but we had each other and, really, that was all that mattered. We could pay rent and we could put food on the table for our children, so we were fine.

There were things about becoming a mother that scared me, and the loneliest time in my life was when I first had Steven. It was just me and this child, alone in the house. I kept myself occupied, cooking and cleaning, but it was hard. I had no mother and no mother-in-law in the country, so when my husband went to work it was just me and the babies. My neighbours and friends really helped at that time. I went back to work when Steven was two years old, at a paper mill. I got to go back to Italy to visit my parents, too, when my son was small. He was the only grand-child my father ever met before he died.

Now I have five grandchildren of my own. I'm lucky because they come to visit me often, though not so much since we've all been in lockdown because of the coronavirus. I'm still happily married. Jovan and I have been married for fifty-nine years. We hardly remember our anniversaries and my husband isn't really the type to bring flowers or be romantic on those days. The romance is in the fact that we are still together after all these years. The romance is in the family we made together, away from the ones we came from. We look after each other. I know what Jovan likes, and I know what he needs. I wash up, he dries the dishes.

We don't go out now because of the restrictions associated with the pandemic. We stay home. And just like my neighbours were there for me all those years ago when I needed support, I am there for mine now. Most days, I get up and I cook lunch for my ninety-four-year-old neighbour. Every day, I cook and clean and wash. I read the paper and I go on YouTube. We watch documentaries about back home in Yugoslavia. My darling husband is sometimes upset seeing them, it can be too hard for him and he becomes emotional. He can't buy pyjamas with stripes on them, for example, because of the concentration camp he was in as a boy.

I've been sewing masks to give to family and friends. My children shop for us and bring us supplies so that we can stay inside and be safe. I'm okay most days. I get anxious and I'm a little bit scared; scared of the world and scared of the virus. I worry for my grandchildren and their future more than I worry for myself and my husband. I tell them to be sensible and to look after themselves. I like to see everybody busy because it's harder to be scared when you're busy. This is not how life should be, how we're living at the moment, but we try to stay positive and we find solace in doing things for other people. I'm happy when I know my kids and my grandkids are safe and busy, working or studying so they can have a bright future.

Immigrating to Australia all those years ago helped prepare me for this time we're living through now with the coronavirus. The hardest thing about physical distancing, lockdowns and self-isolation has been that I'm not free to go shopping or have coffee out like I used to. Or have my family over for dinner. It would be so nice to be all together. So my experiences as a young person who lived away from her family for so long have helped. I am also reminded, a little bit, of how it used to be during the war. The shops are all closed, like they were back then. It feels strangely similar in some ways. Only now I speak English – and I don't eat as much polenta.

Lilia Graovac is eighty-two years old and lives in Ballarat. Lilia shared her story with Kate Leaver.

*'When the coronavirus pandemic
began, I went into isolation early and
decided to work with my brother
and sister on the diaries my father
left behind. This period has given me
an opportunity to know my father
better, to thank him.'*

Carmel Daveson

My father never spoke to me about his experience as a prisoner of war in World War II. Even my mother never knew about it until she saw a documentary later in her life. The only time I ever spoke with my father about his war diaries was when he was dying. He was a stoic person, with a sense of purpose. I was looking for something to help him survive, to keep him alive. I naively thought that if he could get through the war, he would conquer cancer. In the last week of his life, I walked into his hospital room and said, 'Dad, why don't we write up your war diaries?' He was sitting on the other side of the bed with his back towards me, and, for the first time ever, I saw my father's shoulders slump. Without looking at me, he said, 'It was too much to ask of any man.' He turned to face me and continued, 'Kid, if I had to do again what I had to do as an officer, I would kill myself.'

That was the only time in my whole life my father shared any emotion with me. I had never known my father to give up on anything. If you read his diaries, you would understand what a dreadful experience it must have been as a lieutenant and later as an acting captain, being responsible for forming working parties of ill and starving men. The inhumanity his men endured was horrendous and he felt responsible for them. This was particularly true when he worked on the Burma-Thailand railway line. The experience changed him irrevocably. When I reflect upon the impact of World War II on my father, my mother and myself, I can see it was the sense of belonging to a wider community and bigger purpose that sustained us. That period shaped the direction of my life.

I was born in November 1938 in a little country town called Monto in Queensland. My dad was a law clerk and studying to be a lawyer. My mother's role was that of homemaker. I was two and a half years old when my dad enlisted as a private in the Australian Imperial Forces. When he left Australia, his title was Regimental Sergeant Major of the 2/26th Infantry Battalion, the highest-ranking non-commissioned officer in a battalion. Soon after arriving in Singapore he received his commission as a lieutenant and by February 1942 he was a prisoner of war in Singapore.

During the war years, we went to live with my mother's family in a smaller town called Thangool. We survived because that community built a shell around my mother. They were there to support her and to be with her while my father was held prisoner. Women's lives must have been very hard. What pulled us all through was a mindset of, *We will do it together. We will manage together. We will cope.* Our life was one of constant questioning. Dad was gone and we didn't know whether he was dead or alive until the first postcard arrived. It said that he was safe and well and we were not to worry about him. The reality was very different, of course.

In his diaries, Dad wrote about always longing for mail. My father detailed every letter or telegram that had been sent to him, the date it was written and the date he'd received it, which was often two years later. He would have been in the thick of battle when he received the telegram saying that my brother Tyrrell had been born. My mother had never worked for money until my father was a prisoner of war. She was gracious, musical, and seen as very 'feminine'. Hospitality oozed from her. But during the war my mother took herself off to Rockhampton and learned to be a hairdresser. She and one of her sisters also played for country dances. By the time my father came home from the war, my mum had paid off their little house in Monto. She had done it all by herself.

My father's sisters and aunts were strong-minded women who owned and operated small businesses. One of his aunts was the matron of a women's hospital in Toowoomba, and two of his sisters were talented Morse code operators, running the Thallon telephone exchange. I remember my father's aunts as not only strong, competent and community-minded, but as women who did not demonstrate affection easily. I learned from them that how people present to the outside world often hides the real emotions they may be feeling. By contrast, my mother's family were warm, outgoing and demonstrative women. They were similarly involved in their communities. From them I was taught that sharing our 'ups and downs' with others could strengthen relationships and energise us through difficult times.

It was one of my father's sisters who told my maternal grand-father that my father was alive, and on the ship coming home. By that time, my dad had been a prisoner of war for more than three and a half years. I was eight years of age when he came home. My extended family had done their best to keep the idea of him alive for me. They told me he was a determined and clever person who always thought of others. They said he was brave and handsome. So, though I didn't really remember my dad as a physical being, I knew about him and I knew that he loved me. But when my brother Tyrrell first saw my father, he was terrified and ran. You see, Dad was almost a skeleton.

When Dad was discharged from the army, and then the rehabilitation hospital, we returned home to Monto. My mother gave up work, resumed the role of homemaker and gave birth to my sister, Barbara. Dad returned to his earlier occupation as a law clerk. This required an enormous adjustment on his part. Dad struggled to survive, in terms of income, and also being confined to a small office. He was trying to adjust to a normal life, as well as supporting three children. Dad told me that one doctor who examined returned soldiers said that Dad would be dead by the time he was forty. Dad eventually gave up his dream of being a lawyer and became a hotelier instead. He became so well-known and respected that a poem was written about him and his hotel.

The concept of post-traumatic stress disorder didn't exist then. Soldiers were expected to resume their civilian exis-tences and occupations as if nothing had happened. To 'get on with their lives'. Dad continued to suffer from malaria for the rest of his life. I understand he also told my grandmother that he was terrified of having a flashback nightmare of being at war and unintentionally hurting my mother, who was lying next to him in bed. Dad was a disciplinarian. I suspect that leading his men into battle, their surrender, the experiences as prisoners of war, and his determination to survive played a major part in that.

Sometimes in his diaries my dad shows how on edge he was. He writes: *My mind is going. I am weak. I'm not going to manage. How will I survive? I don't know how I've survived so long.* But then he'll say to himself, *Pull yourself together, you must pull yourself together.* You can feel from his words that throughout those dreadful, terrible experiences, he was determined to do what he had to in order to survive and save as many men as he could. He knew if he kept the men occupied then maybe they'd have a chance. That strength of character comes through in those diary entries. My father always had high expectations of himself and others but upon his return home, those expectations became even higher. Particularly in terms of Tyrrell and myself. My dad was determined that we would succeed, that we would never lie and that we would work hard. Once, when I received 99 per cent for a theory exam, Dad asked me what happened to the other mark.

If I'm honest, those early post-war years were difficult, both financially and psychologically. We were still living on rations and my mother used to buy the cheapest cuts of meat and braise them, then carve the roast at our dinner table as finely as paper. But we were brought up with integrity. Dad would say to us, 'Who you are, what you stand for and what you do is what you will be known by. It is not how successful you are, nor how much money you have; it is you, as a person. So, Carmel, when they say your name, "Carmel McGeever", they will know what you stand for. You must never ask someone to do anything you wouldn't do yourself. You must be one with people.'

On the night my sister made her debut in Brisbane at a military event, two men came up to me on separate occasions. Both asked whether I was my father's daughter. I confirmed that I was and one said, 'I want you to know, I hated your father when we were prisoners of war, but I am only here because of him.' The other, who was a colonel, told me, 'If I had had ten more men like your father, I would have brought back thousands more men alive.' I'll never forget their words.

My grandparents lived with us once my father became a hotelier and while I had no formal duties, I did help out around the place. I can set a great table. I'm a hopeless cook but I always knew, even back then, how to anticipate somebody else's needs. If you had been sitting two chairs away from me, you would never have had to ask for salt and pepper or butter or water. My mother taught us to put 'self' last and, throughout my life, most of my work has been voluntary as a result. I recall that Mum would ice all the cakes at family weddings. She would do it for nothing. She and her sisters would also sing and play at major family events. My mother's family were musicians and when I conducted choirs as an adult, I would remember Mum's words, 'Draw forth from the music its inner essence. Always tell the story. Let the written notes and words speak in a way that they have not spoken before.'

In the fifties there was no career path for me, as I was a woman. At sixteen, I was told, 'You have impressive academic results, but law is not a profession for women.' At seventeen, when I was a junior assistant arranging music programs at a radio station, my dad interviewed the manager of that station regarding my career path. Dad was told there was none. He then suggested I seek out a profession with a promotional pathway. I was very upset, not over the lack of a career, but because it meant leaving a job I loved. Lack of opportunities for women was the norm.

In those days, the majority of women accepted that that was how things were. You married and you raised your children. That was our contribution to the world. It was a difficult time for me to learn that, and a mental health challenge. I wanted more than the world was allowing me. That was emotionally limiting. My next job was at the Commonwealth Bank, where I was an 'adding machine operator' but, as a woman, I was never allowed near customers. I eventually went back to night school to obtain my senior certificate and went to university. I yearned to use my brain and work at my profession, but I was captured by the cultural norms of the time. My father gave me the confidence and courage to find my way outside the gender box. I would eventually stand for local government in Mackay. Initially I was the one female on council, surrounded by all those men. By my second term in office, I had been elected the first female deputy mayor of the City of Mackay.

I have experienced considerable social, economic, technological and political change in my lifetime. Women no longer have to resign from employment when they marry. They can stand for political office. They can take out loans, sign documents and purchase material things in their own name. The gap is closing in education and the professions. We are living longer. Many of us no longer have to scrub floors on our knees or have to wash our clothes in a copper boiler. Domestic violence against women is now recognised and we're beginning to understand other subtle and covert ways that women experience violence too. There is still a long way to go. When I was a young woman, I experienced exclusion based on gender and some women still do today. Now I experience exclusion because I am old.

What matters is not the nature of the adversity or the event that is facing me, but the way I cope with that event, both as an individual and with the support of others. My professional practice is facilitating social change with others. I am aware that resilience research has focused on how the individual addresses anxieties and issues. However, it is my experience that when we face adversity together, when we form mutual trusting relationships and seek solutions together, our courage, confidence, skills and belief in ourselves grows. Together, we still need to do more, in any small way we can, if we are to create a more just, inclusive and caring community.

I have certainty that we are constantly changing and every situation, good or bad, makes us the person we are. None of us wants to face upheaval, but let us embrace these challenges together and support each other. This is particularly true in the face of a pandemic like we're experiencing today. My teenage grandchild was wise when she told me that the coronavirus lockdowns were providing our earth with the 'opportunity to breathe again'. I have enormous faith in young people, and wish we older people would listen to them and provide more opportunities for them to make a difference. Young people need to feel that they can bring about change.

When the coronavirus pandemic began, I went into isolation early and decided to work with my brother and sister on the diaries my father left behind. Firstly, typing them out exactly as written and then, secondly, translating them. This period has given me an opportunity to know my father better, to thank him for being the disciplinarian he was, for the high expectations he set and the sense of integrity he instilled in me. People ask me how long the pandemic will go on for, and how long we will be confined to our homes. When that happens, I think about my father, who wrote many times in his diaries, *Will this never end?* His words give me the strength to not think of a time or date for it to all end. Instead, I try to think about what contribution I can make.

Dad never thought my sisters and I should be discriminated against for being female. I always had the feeling with him that I could do anything – whatever I set my mind to. Additional to his example, belonging to a community broader than my immediate family has built my resilience over time. My mother, grandmother, aunts, extended family and some of my lecturers have changed my life. My close friends and colleagues continue to do so. To the amazing women who have come before me, I say, 'Thank you, from the depths of my being.' I believe that, until the day I depart this earth, I will be in the process of becoming the person I am through my relationships with others.

Carmel Daveson is eighty-two years old and lives in Mackay. Carmel shared her story with Emily J. Brooks.

*'Where does my resilience come from?
It comes from my unwavering faith . . .
It comes from my deep love for my
family and friends. It comes from
necessity.'*

Alice Moshi

I was born into an Assyrian Christian family, in the autumn of 1961, in the Iraqi capital of Baghdad. I now live in Sydney's eastern suburbs. I am fortunate to have six daughters, six grandchildren and four sons-in-law, though they are more like sons. My daughters often think I take the boys' side in marital disputes. All my daughters are educated and success-ful which, after the suffering they've endured, makes me very proud. I have prayed for strength. My story is about faith and family and, at times, inconsolable grief. Grief, as you know, is the price of love.

My mother and father, Elishwa and Kirio Ishak, were good people and I was one of eleven children. We had many cousins and friends. When my father asked me if I would like to marry my third cousin, Gillyana, I was pleased. I trusted my father. I married when I was fifteen years old. Do not judge us for this because my father and Gillyana's mother, who arranged the match, only ever acted out of love for us both. My husband was a kind and holy man. To this day, when people mention his name, they cry. He is the only man I have ever loved.

The marriage celebrations went for five days, from Saturday to Wednesday. The afternoons were hot, and they were filled with so much laughter, dancing and drinking. We were happy and I fell pregnant immediately. My first thought was, *Please God, give me a boy*, because I desperately wanted my husband to have a son. The first of my six daughters, Shamiran, was born in 1976. Despite the mix of ethnic cultures and broader tensions in the region, Baghdad was still peaceful at this time. A year later, when I was still only seventeen, my second daughter Susan was born. My sister was a midwife at the hospital and, as you would expect in a big family, I had a lot of help. It was not like it is for families today, where mothers often feel so alone.

Then trouble started brewing. The monster who was Saddam Hussein was growing in power and stature in Iraq. My husband, Gillyana, who was older and wiser, was more aware of Hussein's evil and the potential danger ahead. He was soon conscripted into the Iraqi Army for the second time in his life.

In 1979 I gave birth to Siamese twin boys. I was excited to have boys but because they needed surgery, they were whisked away by my protective sister. One of the babies died almost immediately and the other only lived for eighteen days. I never even saw them. My sister assured me their deaths were for the best.

I was heartbroken. The loss of the twins remains one of the most distressing periods of my life. I was still grieving when the army decided my husband would be stationed in the north. We knew this meant he would be expected to kill the enemy – and most likely be killed himself. He came to me and said, 'Alice,

I love you very much and I love my family, but I have to leave the army and leave Baghdad.'

Gillyana laid out a plan to escape by hiding out in Northern Iraq among the Kurds. My husband proposed we live off the land and I knew it would be a tough life. But what choice did I have? I said, 'I love you and I am going to go with you.' We left Baghdad for the village of Kanibelav in the mountains, not far from the border with Turkey. We had a small house, a cow, horses and some chickens. Our life in Kanibelav meant supporting the oppressed Kurdish people. My husband instructed me to give them food whenever they came knocking. My mother-in-law, who had lost her husband years earlier, came with us too.

This is how we lived for a time. I would spend summer in the village and leave in the winter, with the children, to visit my family in Baghdad. My husband would arrange for his best friend, a young Muslim man named Said Bahjet to drive us in his taxi to and from our hiding place. While we were away, my husband would help people escape by leading them through the mountains into neighbouring Iran and then he would return alone. One time he walked a family of twenty-six people to safety. A year after we moved to Kanibelav, I gave birth to Vivian. It was just as well my husband believed that every baby was a gift from God because in quick succession we then had Nariman, Assourina and the youngest of the family, Domarina.

Meanwhile, Saddam Hussein was losing the war with Iran. The Kurdish rebels had taken advantage of the conflict and reclaimed much of their mountain homeland. In an attempt to exert control, Saddam had begun killing his own people with chemical weapons. To escape these attacks, we would rise before dawn and head into the mountains to hide out in a cave. In 1988, the war with Iran was ending and Hussein had lost. It's estimated he slaughtered 250,000 Iraqis and uprooted more than one million people. In August, along with tens of thousands of others, we were given two hours to flee the village. We were told Hussein's men were on their way and he was threatening to kill us all. We urgently made plans to cross the border into Turkey. I was terrified but believed we would be able to return in a week or two. I was wrong.

Gillyana rigged baskets on either side of our horse while I was still breastfeeding Domarina, who was nine months old. We put two children in each basket, and we carried the fifth. I was still only twenty-seven years old myself. We were separated from my eldest daughter, Shamiran, who was with my family in Baghdad. We left the village at 4 pm, just as it was starting to get cold. There were many women with no husbands, no food, no nothing. Thankfully we had two other horses to carry our food and blankets. But Gillyana was not well; I could see his eyes were swollen and he complained his shoulders ached. When we lost one of the horses, he insisted on finding the animal. Turning to one of his friends, my husband said, 'Brother, can you take care of Alice while I look for the horse?'

When Gillyana came back, he had discovered a baby boy abandoned under a tree. It was not uncommon – many parents were forced to leave babies when they could no longer carry or feed them. Always, it was the youngest left to perish. Gillyana had picked up the baby and, in a stroke of good fortune, had also found our horse. When he caught up to us, he said, 'Alice, you want a son, God has given you a son,' and put the baby in my arms. Of course, we first had to try to find the little one's real family. By nightfall, there were many people sitting around small fires. My husband started yelling, 'Who's lost a kid?' When Gillyana approached the fourth group, someone said, 'It's her son,' and pointed to a distressed woman, who only hours earlier believed she'd left her baby to die. She looked up, rushed over and threw herself at his feet, to kiss them. Gillyana said, 'No, woman, get up,' and he handed her the baby. She said, 'From this moment, you are going to paradise.'

We trekked for five days to reach the border, where we stayed in limbo for a further seventeen days. The world's aid agencies were in disarray as reports of a humanitarian disaster filtered around the world. By now, there were tens of thousands of families without food or water. The rapidly unfolding situation increased pressure on the Turkish government to act. As we waited, not knowing what would become of us, we battled to keep our children alive. We were living under a single tree and the rain was heavy, drenching our makeshift campsite. Gillyana knew a friend who was returning to the village and successfully had him find and bring my mother-in-law to us. One night we put the children to sleep, but it was so wet and we had nothing but a sheet of plastic to protect them. The three of us sat in the rain for hours stretching it over them, careful not to suffocate the girls by hovering it just above their faces.

Sickness and starvation were everywhere. Many people died while we all lived under that tree. Doramina, my youngest, was also near death and by now Gillyana was very sick, though I swear he never once thought about himself. Occasionally he would put his head on my shoulder and close his eyes to rest. I later came to know that he had Graves Disease, an autoimmune disorder, which, if untreated, is fatal. Eventually, the Red Cross arrived with a convoy of open-topped trucks to transport us into Turkey. We climbed aboard alongside 100 or so other refugees and for twenty-four hours bounced along in the truck until we reached the city of Diyarbakir in Turkey's south-west. The aid agencies had thrown up hundreds of tents in the desert but there were not enough for the approximately 17,000 homeless people. We shared with one other family but there was only one mattress allotted to each tent.

Tension in the camp was at fever pitch. To retrieve water, I had to walk a kilometre each way. In a line for food, I witnessed two women fighting. One of them was heavily pregnant. I saw a sick seventeen-year-old boy pass away. The only food we ate came from the back of an aid agency truck and was thrown to us like animals. Children today cry at the smallest thing but my children, who were always starving, never complained – even when the rain and wind ripped open the fragile tents. The eight of us lived like that for four months. Even though we knew God would protect us it was a miserable life. I was sad, angry and scared. We couldn't let the children outside the tent because sometimes it was too wet or it was too hot and there were too many flies. It was like a jail.

In December 1988 we moved into concrete apartments nearby. They were originally built as emergency housing for victims of an earthquake. Each flat had a small kitchen, bathroom and balcony and was approximately 40 square metres in size. There were thousands of refugees assigned to these apartments and ours was home to three families or approximately thirty-six people. We were on the third floor flat, coupled with other Assyrians, and we all got along well. But there was so little space and there was considerable hardship. Poor plumbing meant we would fetch water using buckets. It was the middle of winter and there was heavy snowfall. There was no electricity or furniture and we lived on rations of chickpeas, lentils and bread. All my children caught measles. We were still refugees and surrounded by a fence, so we were restricted in what we could do. We needed permission from the 'office' to go to the hospital.

Gillyana was often in hospital because his illness was rapidly worsening. His symptoms included irritability, which meant he was getting unusually angry. Eventually he took me out onto the balcony to talk in private and said, 'Alice, I am going to die.' I was so distraught I told him I wanted to kill myself. I loved him so much I didn't care. I prayed so hard. I begged God to take me, not him. Ten days after Gillyana told me he was going to die, he fell in the apartment and someone called an ambulance. As he was being carried in a blanket down the three flights of stairs to the waiting ambulance, he raised his head one last time and, looking at the girls and his mother, said goodbye. When we arrived at the hospital in the ambulance, I was so distressed. I cradled his head, sobbing.

Gillyana passed away on 26 May 1989, at just forty-one years old. I was burning inside from grief. Domarina was one and a half years old and I couldn't even take care of her. For five days I couldn't eat. I was dead inside. People begged me to take food. Over and over I asked God to 'please give him back' but my mother-in-law pleaded with me, saying that my husband remained alive in my children. My family in Baghdad heard what had happened and sent a message warning me not to return. They said, 'Keep going, never ever come home. They will bury you and your children alive.' Others told me that I must immediately leave Turkey, but my husband was buried nearby and I couldn't leave him.

On the sixth day I ate something, and on the seventh day after his death we celebrated Mass. Friends had to support me through the prayers, both physically and emotionally. A priest who heard what was happening and was worried about me, came to visit our overcrowded apartment. He had seven girls and a new baby himself. He promised that he would go to my husband's grave and pray for him every Sunday but on one condition: that I leave Turkey. He said bad things would happen to me and the girls if we stayed.

'If you love your husband you must take your girls and go,' he said.

I stopped crying. I knew it was a message from God. I made up my mind to leave and prayed to God to show me the way. The same priest led a fundraising effort and raised 500 Dinar, enough money for us to make another arduous trip, this time across the country to Istanbul and into Greece. My most treasured possession was a photograph of my husband. I kept it close to me in a bag. But on the journey, some desperate people pretended to help us and, while I was distracted, stole my bag with the photograph inside it. At times we were hidden on the back of a truck by bales of hay. At other times we were on foot. When we finally crossed the border into Greece, we were simply offloaded near a train station and left to fend for ourselves.

Where does my resilience come from? It comes from my unwavering faith and the love and closeness I still feel for Gillyana. It comes from my deep love for my family and friends. It comes from necessity. Looking back, arriving in Athens was a turning point, even though our struggle was not over. We would spend many more months penniless in a foreign country, learning the language and looking for work and accommodation. Eventually

I found regular cleaning work and a flat, in the basement of a building that overlooked a fig tree. The landlord gave us a fold-out bed for my mother-in-law. We furnished the flat with gifts or discarded items found on the roadside.

The girls were able to go to school. Today, women have freedom, independence, positive influences and a strong voice. By the time Gillyana died I had developed into a strong, independent woman. I already spoke four languages and in Greece I had to learn a fifth. The best thing to happen in Athens was the arrival of my eldest daughter, Shamiran. My brother and sister flew with her and after two long years we were reunited. We were so happy but for a while poor Shamiran struggled with having not been with her father and her family when he died. It was a hard time for her.

My job was cleaning the house of a wealthy woman, Koula. When it was time for me to move again, she took me to lunch and insisted on giving me US$1000, which I reluctantly accepted, only because she said it was a present for the children. I didn't want to leave Greece but there was an incentive scheme where people could be sponsored to live in New Zealand and my cousin, Elia, was prepared to make the arrangements. Elia was in one of the groups that my husband had helped flee into Iran and he convinced me that we would have a better life in Wellington. We left, this time by aeroplane, to start again on the other side of the world.

We loved New Zealand and settled quickly. As the girls grew, they had their own lives and became independent. Shamiran was the first Assyrian girl to go to university in Wellington and after graduating, in 2000, she and Susan decided to move to Sydney in Australia. Five years later, my mother-in-law and I followed.

It is hard to describe my relationship with my mother-in-law. She was my sounding board and my soulmate. In many ways she replaced my husband. I loved her and we were inseparable. In her final years I was grateful to be able to nurse her, and she died peacefully in Sydney in 2011.

Sometimes, the girls ask if I am sad. But I never feel alone or lonely. I have my daughters. I have never remarried. Why would I? I had a husband and he was the only one I ever wanted. When I am asked how we survived through it all, the loss of the twins, fleeing over the mountains, the camps, Gillyana's premature death, I tell them my source of survival is purely faith. It keeps me humble and strong and it taught me never to give up hope.

Alice Moshi is fifty-nine years old and lives in Sydney. Alice shared her story with Helen McCabe.

'I've led a normal life and helped people along the way when I could. I wouldn't change one bit of it. I've been satisfied in life. I haven't striven for what I couldn't afford.'

Faye Snaith

When I was younger, women would sit around the tea table and talk. They shared their experiences, not only so they could remember the past, but to pass on their wisdom through the generations. Most young ones I know nowadays don't do that. They have a computer on their lap, a phone in their hand or are watching the television. When I tell my grandchildren stories they say, 'I didn't know that,' and, 'You didn't do that!' But I know everything that our family went through and I have a very good memory.

I was born in 1928, after World War I and just before the Great Depression. My father was born in London 'within the sound of the Bow Bells', as they used to say. The Bow Bells are the bells of the church of St Mary-le-Bow, Cheapside, London. To be born within their ring meant you were a Cockney. My grandmother, who worked as an ambulance driver during the Boer War, nursed my grandfather and then they got married. They had two children before my grandfather died young and my grandmother had to bring up the children on her own.

My grandmother was a suffragette who fought for women's rights. At one stage, she chained herself to the gates outside Downing Street and was put in jail overnight. Today, I enjoy taunting my children and grandchildren that they have a jailbird in the family. When my father was a boy he went to a private school with the Duke of Gloucester. He had wealthy French relatives who funded his schooling, otherwise my grandmother could never have managed it financially. My father wanted to join the navy but my grandmother wouldn't let him. She wouldn't sign the papers and so my dad became a bugle boy instead.

Not much later, my dad came out to Australia; he was likely still a teenager at the time. He started with nothing. He landed in Western Australia and had never seen so much sunshine in his life. He was dumped on a farm and, at the time, all he knew about farms was that they had animals on them. Dad slowly worked his way over to Sydney and that's where he met my mother.

My mum's Australian childhood was a religious one. On Sundays, in her family, you didn't do anything. You had a prayer meeting in the morning, and in the afternoon you went around to visit sick neighbours. That's how my mother was brought up, and that's how we were brought up too. My mum was one of twelve children and because her mother died when she was three years old and her father died when she was fifteen, she had to make her own way. She was a dressmaker and after Mum and Dad got married, for a while they had a flourishing dressmaking business. Mum made clothing for the moneyed people of New South Wales and Dad became a sewing machine mechanic. He didn't know anything about them initially, but he taught himself.

My sister Norma came along in 1931, in the midst of the Great Depression. Dad couldn't get work and Mum lost all her clients because no one could afford fancy clothes. It was a bit like events happening now, actually. They decided to come to Victoria, where they heard there was work. Dad got a ride for us with a furniture delivery man. On the way, we pulled up on the side of a river so Mum could breastfeed my sister. We were all breastfed then. There was no formula. You did everything yourself and despite how bad things were, we were optimistic that they would get better. Today is like a repeat of what we went through then, except that nowadays people think they need a lot more. We did all of our own cooking. We grew all our own veggies. I would encourage younger people to focus on what you have, not on what you don't have. And if it's raining, don't go out and get wet!

Our family landed in a little house in West Coburg, Melbourne. Dad had to queue up for a coupon to buy meat. During World War II, the same thing happened again; we would get coupons for sugar, tea and butter. You were only allowed so much per person. Dad didn't have a job, so he went into the city every day on the tram to look for work. He couldn't afford the tram fare though, so he handed his name in on boarding the tram so they could garnish his wages to pay back the fares later. Dad eventually got a job as a salesman for an English firm, Bell's Asbestos. It was a well-known engineering company. That job helped him pay back those tram fares as well as bring up the family. People were honourable then. If you said you'd pay somebody back, you did.

Mum earned money during the Depression by making children's clothing. It didn't matter how poor people were, the children were always cared for. To fix shoes with holes in them, I remember how my dad would buy skins at the sale yards or take the tongues out of my mother's old shoes to patch up ours so they would last another six months. Kids' feet keep growing, and you've got to have shoes. I went to school in very poor circumstances. Yes, we had to be meagre. In fact, a bit scrooge-like. We lived at the end of the West Coburg tram line but we walked two and a half miles down two sections, to save the additional fare.

When Mum couldn't afford butter and didn't have a coupon, we used the dripping that came from the leg of lamb – that we were allowed only once a week, mind you. We loved dripping on bread with salt and pepper on it. Sometimes that was our evening meal. My sister Norma never had new clothes. She always got my hand-me-downs. That frugality has stayed with me. I don't throw anything out. When I have leftovers, I turn them into something else. I iron paper bags to reuse them. I recycle cling wrap by washing it out and pegging it up to dry. I even white-out names on post packs to resend again and again. My youngest sister, the baby of the family who was born a few years later, was different. She got new clothes and was spoiled rotten. Later, if she saw a dress she liked in a shop window, then she bought it! Even though the bill might never get paid. What she wanted, she got. Norma and I are different. Growing up in the Depression left a mark.

I later won a scholarship to high school, and it was an even further walk away. Of course, we couldn't afford the bus fare, but that did turn out to be rather convenient. The man who would become my husband lived near me and he couldn't afford the bus fare either. He used to walk down one side of the street, and I on the other. The feeling was there, but there was no contact between us. Boys and girls weren't allowed to fraternise in those days. The school was divided by a chain link fence down the centre: the girls had one side and the boys the other. If you needed a book, you weren't allowed to converse with one another to share the book. I had a friend who had a twin brother and even they weren't allowed to talk to one another at school.

I suppose you could say we were shy, but it was a nice way to meet your husband. He once knocked on my door and my dad said, 'Who are you?' He told Dad who he was, but Dad said, 'Well, you needn't come sniffing around here, son.' With that, he was off. We later met up again at a church dance. The chap who ended up being our best man – who was sweet on me too, but I wouldn't have a bar of him – kept picking us out and shining a light on us. He knew that we were to be together. He's the god-father to my children now, and I'm godmother to his children.

World War II started while I was still in high school. I'm not blowing my own trumpet but, because I was smart, I finished early. I went out and got my first job with the Melbourne Harbour Trust. They dealt with all the shipping in and out of the Bay. While the war was still on, the Trust was a very secretive company. I wasn't allowed to talk about my work. I wasn't even allowed to tell anyone where I worked. Everything I distributed to the different shipping companies had to be hand-delivered. We weren't allowed to pop it in the post. It was all wartime secrets. We knew about that submarine in Sydney Harbour long before it was publicised, but we were sworn to silence.

The Melbourne Harbour Trust had been purely a man's organisation in the past, but all the men had gone to war, so they had to employ women with credentials. At first, I was a telephonist and I sat in a cubical no bigger than my toilet with another girl named Marie Bruce. If we both wanted to stand, one had to sit down while the other one turned around. It was that small. We screened every call that went through on one of those old-fashioned plug-the-plug-in-and-turn-the-handle switchboards. I think I could still work one of those. I showed promise, so I was later moved to the engineering department when one of the women up there got sick.

I had to do air raid duty on the roof of our offices one night a week. I was only eighteen at the time, so I had to do it with my more senior colleague, Marie, the one who had worked as a telephonist with me. She was only twenty-two, but I suppose she was more 'senior' than I was. We spent one night per week on the roof of the Trust building in the middle of the city. We were given a grey blanket, a pillow and a camp stretcher and asked to lie there and watch for any activity in the air and spot planes. Marie and I became very good friends. She lived in Hawthorn, on the side of the railway track. Her mother had been widowed very early, so she'd had to bring up Marie and her brother alone. When you were in their front room, you had to stop talking while the train went by because it rattled so much. Marie and I became lifelong friends.

Marie died earlier this year. Before then, we would ring each other regularly and we would talk. We would swap recipes. There wasn't a day that went by that my phone didn't ring with Marie or another friend calling me. We kept a very close relationship without living in one another's pockets. Her daughter came over to give me her wheeler when Marie died, which I don't use because I prefer a walking stick. Marie's daughter still looks out for me. She'll do anything I need. She even gets me food for Pussy, my cat, who is twenty. I've got friendships that have not been short-lived. In fact, they've mostly been very long-lived. Those friendships have seen me through the Depression, a world war, raising a family, the loss of my husband and now this pandemic. We've all had upsets and sadness in our lives, but we get through it. We support each other.

Eventually, I left the Trust and got a job at a furniture store. It was better money, and in those days, you had to have money. The store was part of a chain owned by a man who had emigrated from China. I worked for him for years, right up until I was married and even longer. In those days, you didn't go back to work after you were married. You were finished! But he kept me on because I was smart and able to cope with my work. I helped the accountant and became the assistant accountant for the twelve furniture stores. I did that up until the time I had my first baby. Me and figures! I can't go past a row of figures without adding them up. Nowadays, I go into the shop, add up all of my purchases and put the exact money down on the counter. The girls at the checkout ask, 'How did you do that?' I say, 'Well, I just added it up!' Of course, they have to use a calculator. I'm not knocking that because I think progress is marvellous.

I lived at home until the day I got married at age twenty-one. Dad wouldn't let me get married earlier, even though I got engaged at eighteen. My husband went to teachers' college and spent twelve months teaching in the country. He would save up the train fare to come and see me. When we finally got married, we had three children: two boys and a girl. Then nine grand-children and ten great-grandchildren. To think, that all came from a high school romance where we weren't even allowed to talk to each other.

Even though my husband wasn't a builder, he built our house at night and on the weekends. We all helped. We used to work on it in the morning before we went to work and as soon as we came home while there was still daylight. I would cook two or three meals in advance and have them ready. I've always done all my own cooking and still do. My husband gave up teaching because it didn't pay enough and started his own business. I was the accountant, because I had been an assistant accountant in those furniture stores. His company did all the asbestos pipes and piping. Now we know that caused trouble – the asbestos – but nobody knew that then. My husband died at the age of eighty and I've been on my own for over ten years now.

I believe that you're only as old as you feel and what you can cope with. I try not to live in the past but for the future. However, I do have spinal stenosis, which makes things harder. I got that when I was hanging up nappies in my late twenties. We always had cloth nappies, no plastic things or anything. You started off with three dozen nappies, washed them using Johnson's talcum powder and reused them. I was hanging the nappies on the line when a strong wind came up. The line twisted round and twisted me round, but not my feet. It injured my spine. In those days, you didn't go to the doctor. You got over it. If you got a cold, you'd rub Vicks on your chest and go to school with a camphor bag around your neck. Now I try to do everything for myself, but because of that injury I find it hard to manage the vacuum cleaner.

Even with the coronavirus, I've never worried much about myself. I've always been healthy. I've worked hard and eaten well. As the doctor says, I make sure I have plenty of protein, fresh veggies and fruit. I have a banana a day for the potassium.

Nothing fancy. Going out for a cup of coffee and a sandwich with my sister nowadays costs us about what it costs to feed ourselves for a week. That outing is our luxury because we never really had a lot of luxuries. I've never had an overseas trip. I've never wanted one. My sister, who had the money, did four world trips and she would tell me all about them. That's how I had my trips overseas, through her stories and my imagination.

I've led a normal life and helped people along the way when I could. I wouldn't change one bit of it. I've been satisfied in life. I haven't striven for what I couldn't afford. My kids and grandkids have followed in my footsteps – resilient, every one of them. Life requires being reasonable and not asking, 'Why me?' I accept things as they are. I'm not a great one for change. I like things a certain way. Most importantly, I'm a very content person. I'm content with what I have. At the moment I'm sitting here in a nice warm house with both the heaters on, Pussy lying at my feet waiting to be lifted onto my lap, and soon I'll make a cup of coffee, watch the news, and maybe a documentary. I like to know what's going on.

Faye Snaith is ninety-two years old and lives in Melbourne. Faye shared her story with Kristine Ziwica.

'I see the lockdown as a chance for people to experience what it is like to be stuck indoors and unable to enjoy their usual freedoms. My hope is that everyone can come to consider and understand a little more what it is like to live confined by a disability.'

Liz Coles

On the day Alan Bond led Australia to victory in the 1983 America's Cup, I was in Adelaide's Glenelg Hospital. I had recently given birth to my third child, David; a baby brother for Stephen and Nina. When David arrived, he was bathed, wrapped and whisked off to the nursery. I was left to make the most of the bed rest, which was encouraged in those days. Hours after *Australia II* crossed the finish line to snatch victory from America for the first time in the 132-year history of the race, my paediatrician came to visit me in the ward. The paediatrician said he had some test results. The doctors had verified that my newborn son, David, had trisomy 21 – Down syndrome – the most common type of this genetic disorder.

My mind started to race. I was scared that someone might present me with 'options'. The young paediatrician, for whom it was probably the first time he'd had to deliver this sort of news, said that my newborn would never grow up. He told me that I should 'try to love him if you can'. He then handed me the most awful reading material, *You and Your Mongoloid Child*, written in 1963, featuring some severe cases of Down syndrome. I wish I had kept it. Thoughts were flooding my brain like electrical currents. I imagined the voice of my mother saying, 'You gave your baby away?' Would someone ask me if I wanted to give him away? Was this *that* moment? But the worry was unnecessary as no one asked, and I would never have given my baby away.

During the pregnancy I was offered and had refused the amniocentesis, the test for Down syndrome. After David had been born, I wondered what I would have done if I'd taken the test? What if I'd known beforehand? When the paediatrician was done talking he was terribly upset, so I gave him a hug and fare-welled him. I needed to be alone. Once he'd left, I thought to myself, *Well, that's rock bottom, so everything else is up.* I was then moved into a private room, which I didn't appreciate. I felt like we were being shunned. After the nurses brought David to me to be fed, I objected by taking him back into the nursery like the other mums. It was peaceful there. I used the time to think. I like to describe it as 'Why me?' time. But I was actually thinking, *Well, why* not *me? Why would I be so special that it wouldn't happen to me?* I am pleased I had the capacity to think like that, mostly because 'Why me?' assumes it should happen to someone else. I certainly didn't wish it on anyone else.

Those early years were difficult, and I lost a lot of friends. People didn't have time for me anymore. 'How's David?' they would say, wanting me to reply that David was well and every-thing was easy. But I was not going to make stuff up. That would have been wrong. This was David's *life* and I had to be honest about it. I had one friend who came to visit when David was still in the bassinet. She asked, 'Is he healthy?' and I cheerfully said 'Yes! But he's got Down syndrome.' She raced out the door saying, 'I've got to go.' I never saw her again. Perhaps she had some personal experience that made being around David difficult. I don't know. But I missed her. I could have done with her company and support. She was fun; and I really needed a laugh.

There was no paternity leave in those days and, naturally, my husband Phil continued his work. He was an exceptional and dedicated teacher, and I loved being married to a teacher. Past and present students would shout out to him 'Mr Coles!' and breathlessly update him on their lives. A child with a disability can be really difficult for men. We didn't talk a lot about it. If Phil caught me in a dark room crying, I would say, 'It's okay, I'm just having a few tears.' He'd reply, 'Okay,' and leave. I am not sure what he thought, but I felt then as I do now that it's important to have a good cry.

I first met Phil when I was asked to make up numbers at the tennis club. We were playing at the Willaston Methodist courts on a very hot day in December and Phil, who was good at tennis, invited me to sit in his car to escape the heat. He later told me he fell in love with me that day and decided he wanted to marry me. Just like that. For my part, I thought he was quite lovely but I didn't think of marriage. After that summer I returned to boarding school and Phil, who was eighteen and at university, went back to study. He even dated someone else for a while.

A couple of years later we met up again. I was twenty-one by then and eventually we married on a Friday night in January 1974. I knew I wanted to be with Phil. I thought he was someone I could always trust. I walked down the aisle of Scots Church on

North Terrace in Adelaide, wearing a wedding dress I'd made myself. I had three attendants, including my sister Christobel, who was my matron of honour. Throughout our marriage, I found it hard to compete with Phil's work. He was such a dedicated teacher. He took it personally when people suggested teachers were overpaid or lazy. He would often arrive home and work while he ate his dinner. Phil would keep working until eleven at night and start again at dawn. He'd often leave the house before I was even up. Sometimes I resented that, especially when I was left to make big decisions about the family on my own.

Those decisions mostly revolved around David. I knew that if David was capable enough then he needed to be integrated into the mainstream education system. It remains the case that children with special needs perform significantly better when integrated into mainstream classrooms. However, this was unfashionable thinking back then. Eventually, the state government announced new laws that moved away from institutional care and enabled mainstream integration with some support.

When David was little, I started to write everything down. At first, I wanted to capture the joyful stuff about David because he had such a wacky personality. He was such a gem, really. It was also one of the ways I coped. I would wake up at night and write all my thoughts and feelings down. This really helped. It also gave me a record of events, especially when doctors asked me questions.

David was allowed to 'visit' the local kindergarten. The first kindergarten was unwelcoming, so we moved. Then one day, when he was only three, I went to move a chair for him so that he could take part in a game of bingo. The teacher tried to stop me by saying, 'This will be too hard for you, David.' I bit my tongue and pushed in his chair anyway so he could have a go. I am good at biting my tongue, though as I get older it's been getting harder. As it turned out bingo was David's specialty.

Often, as a little boy, he would try to keep up with classmates. He would fail at first but then he would surprise everyone and get it. You never knew where he would struggle and where he would succeed. We had to experiment. We had to keep at it. We had a similar early experience at primary school. David was treated poorly by his first teacher, who resented him being in her class. She didn't even assign him a desk, saying, 'He doesn't sit down very much, anyway.' That meant David would often miss the start of class, partly because he loved having the slippery dip to himself.

That teacher would only give him the most basic books to read, when in fact he was quite a good reader. When she wasn't around, I would slip into the class and swap his books for something more challenging. An early intervention teacher went to evaluate what was happening and she rang me, sobbing. She said the way he was being treated by the school was horrific. But she also warned me to be careful because they would kick David out if I made too much of a fuss. Thankfully, the next year he was assigned a new teacher called Nancy. At first, I thought she was too good to be true. I'd never experienced a teacher being that nice to David. It gave rise to emotions I initially didn't recognise because it was the first time since David was born that I didn't feel fear. David no longer spent the start of class alone on the slippery dip and Nancy became a lifelong friend.

'Mum, will I be going to Brighton High or not?' David started to pester me. He wanted to know if he'd be attending the same school as his siblings. I would say, 'I don't know, we will have to see.' For Stephen and Nina, my other children, disability has always been a part of their lives so they have grown up with strong awareness. They are thoughtful and understanding, but I'm not sure they learned that from me. Life has been their teacher. Eventually, when David was old enough, the principal did welcome him to the school. It always made me so proud to see him walk through that gate.

Some of the students at high school had gone to kindergarten with him, so they knew and enjoyed David's company. After school one day I arrived and I could hear David on the footpath loudly singing 'Jingle Bells'. It was the middle of June. I saw other kids smiling as they passed, saying, 'Hi Dave,' and giving him a high five. I was a bit embarrassed but then I felt proud of him and of the other students for their acceptance of him. That was a nice moment.

David was nineteen when he graduated from Brighton High, with his Year 12 leaving certificate. By this time, everyone there knew and accepted him. In his final years of school, I encouraged him to do work experience. We had some disheartening attempts, including a stint in a library, stacking toilet paper at Coles and washing dishes at a restaurant. Inevitably, I would be summoned to the office to be told, sometimes in great detail, why he was unsuited to the work. Eventually, David found work he really enjoyed at the Down Syndrome Society office: collating, stapling and packing envelopes.

I don't know if I was resilient, but I know I always stood up for David. I would visualise myself on one of those obstacle courses you see in an advertisement for army recruits, determined to find a way up or over. When I was challenged by well-meaning people about my decisions I would say, politely, that I was doing what was best for David. When I was told David couldn't do something, it often just needed some direction and practice. I would quietly set about proving them wrong. I wish that I could experience what it's like to have Down syndrome for just two weeks. I always wished I could better understand it from David's perspective. There are also a few doctors I wish could experience what it is like.

David is now in his thirties and, instead of schools, I am battling the National Disability Insurance Scheme. In 2017 he was diagnosed with Multiple System Atrophy, a rare degenerative neurological disorder affecting the body's involuntary functions, including blood pressure, breathing, bladder function and motor control. I took care of him until it became too much. Today he is in a motorised wheelchair and in full-time care in North Adelaide. It was like his life had unravelled. David lost his ability to walk, speak and to use his hands. Skills he had learned were lost. I visit a few times a week, mainly to read to him, so he's not always left in front of the television.

In the meantime, I have also had to adjust to a life without Phil, my husband. I had suspected Phil was suffering from dementia as early as 2008 but it took a couple of years to get a diagnosis. My father had died from dementia-related health issues. I recognised the signs and I started to make a record of peculiar things Phil said and did. The doctors insisted on testing him for multiple other conditions, including depression. Eventually I was proved correct.

For seven years I took care of Phil, but he was 6.5 ft and he could get angry. He always hated being a passenger so I would be quite anxious when we were in the car together, fearing he would snatch the wheel in his frustration. I was also tired and after managing David's incontinence, I didn't think I could do that for a second time. And, just as I knew I was not too special to *not* have a child like David, I also understood I wasn't immune from another challenge. I always understood, in life, your number goes back into the barrel. You can never predict what it has in store. You don't know where all the roads lead and even a pretty road can lead to a steep cliff.

I thought I could take care of Phil but I was naive. Until you have lived with dementia twenty-four seven you can't know what it's like. Over the years I had found friendship and support from a group of Down syndrome mothers. So when things with Phil started to wear me down, I joined another support group. The first day I turned up as the new person and, after a few stories and raucous laughing, I felt a lot better. I found both support groups helped. They prepared me for the worst, but mostly we just laughed and shed a few tears. Phil was admitted to residential care in 2015, aged only in his sixties. There were days when he was surprisingly lucid, and he would come back to me. One day he asked if we were young lovers, and I said, 'Oh yes.' Over the next two hours he stood facing the window, mostly with his eyes shut, while I recounted the story of our lives. He gently rubbed my hand and just listened. It was such a special time. I remember thinking I was getting to give him his eulogy. Most people don't get to hear their eulogy. He died a few days later.

Giving birth to a child with a disability gave me a wonderful perspective on life. It was as if I could see the world in another dimension, and it was a universe mostly unknown or unexplored by others. To most people the solitary child on a school slippery dip was invisible. But to me? That person needed and deserved to be cherished. Think of it as viewing life through a piece of distorted Perspex and when the plastic is removed, there's clarity. I hope the experience of the pandemic helps others see what I do: that many people with a disability cannot go outside or even move rooms without assistance; or can find themselves stuck in front of a television, watching a show they might not even like.

I see the lockdown as a chance for people to experience what it is like to be stuck indoors and unable to enjoy their usual freedoms. My hope is that everyone can come to consider and understand a little more what it is like to live confined by a disability. If I am pushed to give advice to people feeling a bit lost or alone I would say: stay connected to friends, and continue with a fitness regime and hobbies as best you can. Other people have challenges to deal with; big or small, they are still challenges. Learn from other people how they deal with situations – watch, ask, listen. And, finally, manage the amount of negative information you hear or read, especially about the coronavirus.

I am not sure if my story is about resilience. What I do know is that whenever my number came out of that barrel I tried to do my best.

Liz Coles is sixty-eight years old and lives in Adelaide. Liz shared her story with Helen McCabe.

'I tell people that this is a very hard time at the moment . . . It's important that we honestly share those feelings with each other.'

Dorothy McRae-McMahon

I was born on the west coast of Tasmania in 1934 but I left there in a cardboard box lined with material three weeks later. My dad was a Methodist minister. I can remember being three years old and having a sense of another presence around me, a comforting presence. I always felt there was something beyond me. In those days, ministers and their families were moved around every three years. It was hard on the kids. I was the eldest of five children: three daughters and two sons. My sister Carmyl managed to keep in touch with her friends each time we moved, writing letters and calling them on the phone. I wasn't sure what to do and felt I had to make new friends every time. I became quite lonely.

My dad wasn't a fundamentalist. He didn't believe in every word of the Bible; rather, he thought you should reflect on it quite deeply. He had degrees in religion and philosophy. Dad was a radical minister who was politically and staunchly anti-racism. I never had to unlearn anything he taught me because he was loving and open-minded. My mother, on the other hand, was a more conservative Christian. I had a lot of difficulties with her over the years. She left school at age twelve, after both her parents died, and became a milliner. Mum was also a healer, who would lay her hands on people and pray for an end to their suffering. People were amazed by her skills and many would ask for her help.

Being a minister, my father was a pacifist and initially refused to go to war. Eventually, though, the public shaming became too much. People put white feathers in our letterbox and that got to him. He felt he was betraying the family and bringing shame on us. He also felt he might be able to make life more comforting for the soldiers if he did go to war. The night before he left, he gathered the three eldest children and stood us in front of him. He said, 'Now, girls, I may never speak to you again because I may never come back. And so I want you to always remember what I say. You are not to do like others and say horrible things to the bottle-o.'

He was referring to men, usually of Asian descent, who would go about collecting empty glass bottles and selling them back to the manufacturer for a small amount of money. Racist things would be said to them in the community. Dad continued, 'You're not ever to think of anybody of another race as less honourable, less important or less significant than you.' He was away at war for two years. I missed him so much.

At the height of the war we were living in Hobart. This was where the big warships were sent for servicing and refuelling. It also made Hobart a potential target for the Japanese and so we dug trenches at our primary school. When the alarms would sound, the children would go and sit in the trenches and put bits of rubber between our teeth. The adults were worried that if a bomb came down we might clench our teeth and hurt our mouths. If the air raid alarm went off when we were at home, there were black curtains that would be pulled down to cover the windows. It was thought this would stop low flyers from seeing the houses and dropping bombs on us. We felt terribly afraid whenever those alarms would go off, as if these might be the last moments of our lives.

We were a poor family because ministers of religion weren't paid much at all. We didn't have a car and had barely enough to keep us alive. We were hungry. Meat was a rarity, and even when we had some it would only be a small mouthful. The other kids had two shillings per week for pocket money and we only had a penny each. We would save it up to get threepence-worth of lollies at the shop, but we couldn't afford birthday presents for friends or anything like that. I felt alienated from other kids because our family was more hard-up than theirs. Our school uniforms were always second-hand and didn't fit very well. I used to wear my aunt's old clothes which was rather embarrassing. I am eighty-six now and I love shopping. I just love it. Even going to Coles to get the food. I do it every day!

Dad taught us to be genuinely concerned about other people. Justice was important to him, in both his preaching and in his parenting. He would tell us that people who truly cared didn't just care in their heads, they did something about it. Then, in the early years of high school, I was invited to take part in a debate about the White Australia policy. I very much wanted to be part of it but felt too scared. I was a nervous child and rather shy at that time. Dad told me that when I cared enough about something, I would find my voice – and I did. I went and I debated. They could never stop me after that.

I became a preschool teacher in Geelong after three years of training, and that was where I met Barrie McMahon. I was twenty-one, he was twenty-two and together we had four children. My first child, Christopher, was a lovely, bright little boy who became severely brain-damaged as a four-year-old. I believed in vaccinations and I still do, but it was sadly a very rare reaction to the polio vaccine that caused Christopher's disability. He became incredibly wild and would run off down the street and scream and lash out. People would look at us, but I have always felt comfortable in explaining what was happening. I would say that I was sorry and that this was simply something we had to deal with. Mostly people respected that.

I gave Christopher my life for sixteen years but he eventually became difficult to manage and needed twenty-four-hour care. He had grown bigger than me and I knew I had to ask others to help. We put him into care for young people in similar circumstances. Otherwise, he may have ended up in an aged care facility not suited to his age or needs. I felt all right about it because I had given him everything I had and that was all I could do. It was time for other people to help me care for him. He was given medication once he was in care and he calmed right down, becoming a quiet and gentle sort of person. Finally, I could live again. I had freedom and time to pursue what mattered to me. And it was around that time I began to think maybe I was married to the wrong person. I wasn't attracted to Barrie anymore, not sexually. He noticed it as well. Of course, it wasn't that he was the wrong man. It was that I was a lesbian.

In those days I didn't even know the word homosexual. I eventually became aware of a group of feminists who met in various pubs and I joined them. I began to realise they were in love with each other and were in partnerships and so on. I began to think about that more and more. Then in 1985 I met a woman called Jenny Chambers at a party and we had a certain attraction. She said to me, 'Are you a lesbian?' I said, 'No.' She replied, 'Well, you should be!' I came to realise that I was and I began telling people who were close to me. By doing that I really did put everything at stake – my work, my ordination and my family. I had stepped off the cliff and instead of falling, like I had expected, I began to fly. I felt truly alive and completely myself for the first time. I could be who I was.

I was still married to Barrie, of course, and had to break the news to him that I was a lesbian. He found it hard and we both grieved the end of our marriage, but he did accept it. He was very generous when I ended the marriage. We remain friendly to this day. He sold the house and all his shares and gave me half the value of both. Legally, he did not have to do that. My children also supported me, and I recall that one of them said, 'About time, Mum!' If there is one reason that I am glad I didn't know I was a lesbian earlier in life, it is my children. I am grateful for them and I now have three grandchildren too.

Before my marriage ended, I had received a call from God. I began my training for a Diploma of Theology to become a minister just like my father. I was ordained when I was fifty years old and asked to be the minister at the Pitt Street Uniting Church in Sydney. In 1983, when I arrived, the congregation only had seventeen members and they were thinking of pulling the church down. Over the ten years I was there we added two hundred new members. The church still stands and even now when I see it I feel proud. It's locked up at the moment because of the pandemic but I will be carried out of there when

I die; my funeral will be there. It's a city church so I have gone in now and again over the years to meditate and I can feel the love we all shared with each other as a congregation. There is such a sense of belonging in the prayers.

I have always felt strongly about human rights. I've been part of a lot of big movements because of the era in which I have lived – the anti-White Australia movement, the peace movement, the anti-Vietnam War movement, the anti-apartheid movement, the women's movement. During the 1980s, neo-Nazis had been writing graffiti all over Sydney that was terribly racist. Our church congregation made it our business to have it wiped out, and that was when some real trouble started for me.

When we found 'Kill an Asian a day' painted in the Stanmore railway station pedestrian tunnel, we asked the council to have it painted over. They said re-painting happened around every six months, and we decided it couldn't wait that long. We tried to paint over it ourselves and were caught by the police. They took down our names and addresses. That was when the neo-Nazis realised who it was that had been painting over all their graffiti. They marched into our church service wearing swastikas, and placed a horrible letter on the communion table. The neo-Nazis, having somehow got hold of my private information, started following me home from church. I lived alone. They would sit in their cars and watch me. They would threaten me verbally and ring my phone in the middle of the night. They even placed a life-sized effigy of a woman on my doorstep and set it alight. It was truly terrifying and it went on for over a year.

Members of the congregation would come and stay with me overnight sometimes. They sustained me. They would pray with me and care for me and they held me, literally and metaphorically, in their arms. My faith never wavered at that time, or ever. It has always been part of my being, right from the very beginning, going back to when I was a little child. There have been times of hardship, but I have always felt this presence of a loving God. The police knew what was happening but didn't intervene. On one occasion the neo-Nazis painted LESBIAN SLUT across the front of my house in the middle of the night. My son Bertie came around the next day and painted over it for me. He said, 'Mum, I will paint out "slut" but I am not going to paint out "lesbian" because I am proud of you.' He is a dear, Bertie.

In 1992 I fell in love with a Kiwi woman called Ali Blogg, a nurse who I met at a party. She was the love of my life. Yes, I was sexually attracted to Ali but when I first met her we just found ourselves talking and talking and talking. We had a deep connection and the relationship happened almost immediately. I fell for her on all fronts. Ali helped me see I couldn't be totally gracious and good to everybody all of the time. She invited me to mature and be more open to consider the more difficult parts of life. I have since learned to look at whoever was being nasty to me and set that aside. I have every right to be respectful of the human journey and not hate anyone, but I also know not to give those people power over me. Ali was so wise and would hear me – and heal me – through her listening and sympathy. Everything about her, I loved. I still do.

I was the first woman to be ordained into the ministry in Australia. There has been a huge shift in my lifetime for women; an increased respect for women and our rights to enter life more completely. The most important shifts have been the right to express what you are thinking about life and do things that have significance. We used to march through the streets for our rights. I am happy to see that women have taken their place in all sorts of ways now. I had already been ordained by the time I met Ali. I had also been elected to the governing body of the Uniting Church, the National Assembly. I knew by then that Ali was the love of my life. I felt I couldn't *not* tell the church about who I was. I was not ashamed. I wanted to honour Ali as my beloved partner.

I can remember being at the Assembly and thinking, *I'd better tell them now*. I stood, with my whole body trembling and my voice trembling too. I wanted to live my life in truth and stand up for other lesbians. When I came out, my parish at the Pitt Street Church gathered me in with all the approval and love you could possibly imagine. It was very special. We had been doing a lot of pastoral work with people living with HIV, because an AIDS diagnosis was fatal in those days. I would visit them in hospital, write blessings for them and then, often, take their funerals. They all stood behind me and supported me. It was a progressive church and still is. I was most fortunate.

Today, our church life has been locked off by the coronavirus. We have a service on Zoom every week but it's not the same as being there together. I tell people that this is a very hard time at the moment. We're all threatened, the whole world is threatened, and we cannot see how we will get past it. It's important that we honestly share those feelings with each other. It is a worrying time and we must find ways of caring for each other in all of that.

When marriage equality passed in parliament, Ali and I did talk about getting married but decided it wasn't for us. We were together for twenty of the most wonderful years. We went on holidays and to concerts, restaurants and movies. We did everything together. I have had a lot of kindness around me in my life and Ali's love was the most precious of all. Then Ali was diagnosed with brain cancer and she didn't last long afterwards. She taught me so much. Ali used to say, 'I am a person of faith but not of the Church,' and she did think I was sexy in my clerical collar. I miss her conversation and the everyday of being together; the fun we would have sharing each other's company. Being raised a Methodist, I had never really had a drink before meeting Ali but now I have a gin and tonic every night – and I rather enjoy it.

Ali showed me how to be more human and acknowledge that I couldn't do everything all the time. Resilience means having the strength to stay present in whatever is happening, including things that take your energy and make you feel stressed. Part of my upbringing, by a father who was a Methodist minister, was that we should always do what was asked of us. To give, even when we didn't feel we could. Ali taught me not to be sacrificial all the time. She would tell me that I should respect myself, that I was not God, I was a human being who should respond honestly and authentically.

My dad, when he was alive, could see that I had learned from and listened to him. He would have been proud. I learned courage from my father. I have always felt that it's important to use my voice for things I believe in and I have done that in many ways throughout my life. We used to have 100,000 people at marches I attended but these days you're lucky to get twenty. I would make banners; I had banners for every cause that mattered to my heart. I was always writing letters to editors. There weren't so many women writing in those days. I won the Australian Human Rights Medal in 1988 and received an Honorary Doctorate of Letters from Macquarie University in 1992. This sort of social justice work lifts your heart and makes you feel more alive. It gives you purpose.

My life has been given a deeper meaning through fighting for equality. Even when you don't achieve all you hoped you would, it feels as though you are living significantly. That work has been rewarding. It has profound meaning for me and has made me feel truly alive. I don't look to whether people are Christian or not; I care about what's in their hearts. There are many pathways in life – and faith was mine.

Dorothy McRae-McMahon is eighty-six years old and lives in Sydney. Dorothy shared her story with Jamila Rizvi.

'I think this moment in history could see us negotiate a new, more peaceful way to live on this land. We can't undo the past, but we can change how we make sense of it. The challenge is for us to see ourselves differently in the world.'

Audrey Fernandes-Satar

My family are originally from Goa, but through the process of the colonisation of India, people were moved off the lands and my family moved to Pune. In Goa, my family had worked on the land, but the British colonists put so many fees and restrictions onto local farmers that it was hard to continue farming. My family left the land and went over to India. I was born there, in Pune, and was one of eight children. I'm number three. The first five of us were born in Pune and numbers six, seven and eight were born in Mozambique.

Our family's house in Goa is still clear in my mind. I feel an enormous connection to that place. The wooden house was at the base of a mountain. In front of the house was a big, thick white cross about a metre high. We used to play around it, never understanding the symbolism. It was the ultimate representation of colonial power, indicating that the people in the house were Catholic and this was a converted house. There were cashew trees and jackals slinking around. Next to the house was a Chikoo tree that I used to climb. It's called Sapota in English. Nanna taught me how to listen to the voices of the birds and to know what kinds of birds they were and why they were singing in the evening.

It's all gone now. I went back almost fifty years to the day since we left, and it had all been mined. The mountain was just a hump of sand. It's difficult to find words to explain that grief. To discover that those trees and animals were gone was an immense hurt and loss to me. It's taken me decades to understand the colonial project and what it takes away from those of us in the diaspora. There's no map that will ever take us back to the things we have lost. After the abolition of slavery, workers were needed across the globe. A lot of Indian people moved to other countries – a whole sea of people crossing the Indian Ocean – to work as indentured labourers. They moved to places like South Africa, Mauritius and all across Africa. This is how my father ended up in Mozambique.

There was a strong recruitment drive and we had other family members living in Mozambique already. Like most people in that position, we thought we were just going for a little while to make some money and then we'd come back. That didn't prove to be the case. We left in 1959. I was five, turning six, and still have a photograph of myself as a little girl on the day we left. I didn't have anything with me besides two little plastic toys. I remember being on the ship leaving Goa. We called the Indian Ocean *kala pani*, which means 'the black water'. I saw that water and got scared and didn't want to get onto the ship. I thought I was going to fall in. I was only a child. I didn't realise that I would never live in India again.

At that time, Mozambique was a colony ruled by the Portuguese under a fascist government. When India took Goa back from the Portuguese by force in 1961, two years later, things became a lot tougher for us. We were classified as people who were treacherous, as 'snakes in the grass'. They thought we were sneaky, hiding and biding our time to do bad things. We had no intention of doing any harm, of course. I was devastated, because we were good people. The political situation had an impact on what happened in school for us kids. I was an eight-year-old child and so many things had changed in my life. My father lost his job and we became very poor because he couldn't get work anywhere else.

My family went to live in the capital, which is called Maputo. There, I developed a strong understanding of racism. The colonialists had these filthy words they'd call us. One of the things that hurt me most as a child was walking home from school with my mum, and I'd hear people calling her those names. It was difficult because what you hold inside of you, your identity – someone was saying it wasn't true or real. There were some words that I couldn't understand because of the language gap but I knew by the sounds of them that they were horrible and negative. When they were shouted out, you felt as if you were naked in the street, stripped of everything. I don't think there are words in the dictionary to actually describe how those behaviours affected my family. It is not in the realm of language.

In my mind I always kept up a kind of resistance. I still do today. I think that came from my mother. She would say very little, but her resistance was demonstrated in the way she conducted herself. I understood that she didn't have to make a noise to protest. The system made us feel like we were inadequate, insufficient, lacking in something. My mother would always insist that we were not lacking, that we had a history. She'd tell us not to forget who we were. Through my mother's strength, I learned to reassure myself. I would never accept that I was inferior. The more I learned at school, the more I understood that the colonialists who despised us were wrong. I learned to be subversive and pursue the truth of histories. For me, education was empowerment but also my form of protest.

I was usually ignored in class and sat right up the back. The teacher had to give me an exercise book because I didn't have one. It had margins in it and I would do my work and then draw in the margins. I illustrated everything that we were studying. The teacher never gave me feedback but I knew I was doing good work. There were days when the government minister would come to the school. The teacher would put all the exercise books on her desk for the minister to go through and I saw mine at the top. I thought, *You don't want to tell me but I know that I am really good at this.*

Though I took pride in learning, I do remember being ashamed of the house where we lived. It was a kind of slum, with holes in the floor. In the evenings, rats would come in. Sometimes at night I'd try to stay awake because I thought they would climb on me. The smell was terrible. The house had no electricity connected and other people lived there too. We didn't have proper shoes. Our shoes had no soles, no bottom. You had to be very careful with those shoes, to make sure your pinkie toe didn't poke out when you went to school. I didn't want anyone to notice how poor we really were. Everything had to be planned and divided. Food, clothing; everything had to go into smaller bits. Mum sewed it all herself. I was aware of the difficulties for my mum but she always found a way. She would cook soups with very little but they kept us going.

We had family in Maputo who were quite well off. My mum used to ask them for money to help when school started. I was quite worried that we wouldn't get the minimum amount needed for me to stay in school. I remember my mum's humility in trying to tell my uncle that we would somehow pay him back. He wouldn't even come inside because he felt that our house was not proper enough for him. He dumped the money in Mum's hand and turned around and closed the door. I spoke to Mum about it years later, to thank her. She started to cry. She didn't know I'd witnessed that event. I told her it made me want to be the best student in school because I knew what was riding on it. I knew that education meant I could get a better job and be able to help my family.

I went to school every day with nothing in my hand. I didn't have a pencil, a bag, a book, but I wanted to learn everything that happened there. I don't remember the teachers ever giving me a grade for my work, such was the intensity of racism in our community. My siblings and I would often get accused of stealing things, which we never did. My mother instilled in us that you must get an education in order to succeed. Education is something that I value and hopefully I've passed this on to my children because it is really important. I've had a cycle of remaining an outsider and having to use protest and having to act out and speak up. Hopefully that cycle has come full circle.

Gradually my parents became a bit better off. They started a furniture business and things changed for me when I began middle school. At night, I would sit at the corner of the street under the streetlight to study and draw. We didn't have power at home. One time, a teacher saw me drawing outside. She recognised that I had talent and waived the school fees so I could study art. Her name was Dona Conceicao. She changed my life. Dona gave me opportunities in art and faith in myself because she believed in me. Once I started teaching myself, I saw how teachers facilitate change. Dona told me, 'You can be good at art, but you need to be good at all the other things and this is how you will get to university.' When you tell a twelve-year-old that, it's like a map for the future. I knew exactly where I wanted to go. I wanted one of three scholarships that were given out each year to study in Lisbon.

I knew I needed really high marks. At that time, the marks in each subject were counted out of twenty. In art I was top of the class. I got nineteen out of twenty. As a result, I did receive acceptance to Escola Industrial, which is the equivalent to TAFE in Australia. However, the head of the Arts College called me and said that he wouldn't allow an Indian to have high marks, especially when white Portuguese students hadn't done nearly as well. He rounded my grade down, so it was just one point above the next highest grade. My score dropped to fourteen out of twenty overall. In one fell swoop I could no longer apply for the scholarship. I sat on the steps in front of the school and cried. I couldn't bring myself to tell my mother what had happened.

I would not give up on my dream, however. I figured out an alternative. I could take exams for entry instead. For the exams you were assigned a number and the results then came out printed on big sheets. That way, no one would know my name or heritage. My family didn't have the money for the exam entrance fee, so I borrowed it from an aunt, and paid her with an artwork.

I'm not sure if it was my resilience that got me to art school and through everything beyond – because that suggests life can throw anything at me and I will overcome it. I don't think it's like that. The people who are doing the throwing need to be accountable. It's not just about the survival of the oppressed but is about undoing the triumph of the oppressor. I do believe that vulnerability can give you space for resistance.

I worked harder than ever to get top grades in the exams, bringing a scholarship application back within my reach. On the application forms, I simply stated that I had Portuguese nationality. This was untrue. I didn't have any nationality at all because none of my family had official documentation. Thankfully, no one checked. I was given a scholarship to art school from a fascist government who didn't even see me as a citizen. Isn't that ironic? I enrolled at the prestigious Portuguese art school Escola Superior Belas-Artes da Universidade de Lisboa, which is the University of Lisbon. We worked long, hard days and the schedule was gruelling. We had to maintain our marks to keep the scholarships we had won. One hundred and fifty of us started that year, and only twenty-nine graduated five years later. I was one of those who did.

It was hard to adjust to that life. The city was grey and noisy. There was so much traffic and not much sunshine. The cobblestoned streets in Lisbon were difficult to walk on and the school was up a steep mountain. I didn't have the best clothes or shoes for winter either, so my feet were often waterlogged. I didn't have many friends. Firstly because I didn't have a lot of time. I was always working and studying. But the social scene in Lisbon was also very different to Mozambique, where I came home to a family and a mother who cooked my meals. In Lisbon people socialised a lot in cafes and you needed money to do that. At the age of twenty-one, I was really unrehearsed in any social relationships.

I was shown my room in the college accommodation. I didn't know how to put on the heater. I froze for a couple of nights until I had the courage to ask someone. The scholarship barely paid for my fees and my food and didn't cover my transport or materials. I started work at a bean factory, literally counting red kidney beans, to cover costs. I worked twice as hard as others because I knew if I dropped the ball, if I missed one class, there would be no excuses. I couldn't afford to make mistakes. It gave me focus. I was judged at university. I always had to prove myself. Both race and gender bias came into play. *How could someone like you be doing a degree like this?* There was only one male student from Africa in the whole of that art school, and no other people of colour.

In 1974, there was a revolution in Lisbon and the fascist government fell. I returned to Mozambique to find much civil unrest. Part of the city was burned. My family's home was in front of a bus stop where a bomb went off on a bus, setting the front of the house on fire. It was the last straw; my father decided that the family could not continue living there. His plan was to come to Australia but due to migration restrictions he went to East Timor instead. To penalise Mozambique, Portugal terminated all the academic scholarships it had granted. However, I was lucky: I had free accommodation and some work that allowed me to finish my degree. I ended up staying in Lisbon for thirteen years, and I met a man. It became a terrible, violent situation and I don't want to talk further about him except to say we had two children together.

After we separated, I met another artist from Mozambique in 1983 called Arif. Arif and I were friends first; he would help me with small things around the house. Then his kindness and solidarity developed into something more. We decided to come to Australia to escape the situation in Lisbon and the political turmoil in Mozambique. I spoke a little bit of English but Arif and my kids – who were five and six at the time – didn't speak any. We weren't married when we emigrated, but there was a lot of trust and love between us. There still is. We had our youngest son here in Australia. It hasn't been easy being on the other side of the world, and yet I have found a peace here that maybe I would not have had anywhere else. Australia is the one place I felt I belonged.

We settled in Perth and I was eager to get a job as a teacher. I assumed it would be the same as in Lisbon and my high marks would mean I'd get a good job. But while my Portuguese qualifications were accepted in Australia, it wasn't a transparent process. The man from the education department who spoke to me was rude and dismissive. He didn't even look at me or ask me to sit down. I'm sure this was because I'm a person of colour. Much later, I discovered my application to teach in Australia was never processed. It was archived. I now believe this was done deliberately. I was rendered invisible.

Since we've lived in Australia, I've observed this kind of practice many times. There is a covert kind of racism. You carry your culture always on your shoulders because of the stereotypes people have of you. But an oppressor's power is not eternal. There's resistance in our vulnerability too. My mother taught me that. It's not passive. It is active. Vulnerability gives agency. As a person of colour, I have always felt I had to be much more accountable, much more knowledgeable and much better equipped than anyone else – just so I could do the same jobs and get the same promotions others get.

People don't want to talk about this reality. They think I bring these things up because I want them to feel guilty or that I like to talk about it. Sexism is layered on top of racism. Why aren't more women in positions of leadership? Why are women still earning much less than men, and we women of colour less again? Why are we still in this position, battling things that people don't even see as prejudice?

I have felt angry at times and have given myself permission to be angry. There is a sense in Australia that if people react to a racist act, then it's because we're inherently angry and violent people. But there is a difference between anger and violence. If I'm confronted with racism, why can't I be angry? I can't be complacent and say that I'm not. There's this myth that black people are violent as a group when really we are simply reacting to racism. We need to talk about racism more. It has had a huge impact on my life and it's important for me to say it. My anger is an active anger. I can't walk away without saying something. Because if I'm silent, I'm complicit right away. I stand in my anger and say, 'I will not accept this.'

For years, I did a lot of cleaning in leafy rich suburbs. Arif was working in a bottle shop and we rented and rented. We didn't have enough money to buy a house back then. I forced myself to learn English fast by using dictionaries and making lists of words for practice. After about four years I did teach in part-time jobs at high schools. One wonderful female principal really encouraged me. I now have three grandchildren too, which is a joy. I have completed a PhD in Perth, researching the history of diaspora, and now work as a lecturer. There is power in what I'm doing, in being seen. I encourage my students to question, to analyse the things that impact their lives and to make meaning of 'facts' in a way that will uncover power structures.

It has taken the pandemic to actually bring out all of this. We are at a turning point. We cannot allow now for this to go back to 'business as usual'. The pandemic has meant we have had to change how we do things. My university has a large number of international students. There have been lots of job losses and our library had to close. I think the change in fees for arts students is a travesty. How are we to imagine a world without the humanities? Without the knowledge, the experience, the dreams, the inspiration that those units bring? What would I have been without my arts degree? I don't think we can imagine a world without this. I think we should all be very, very concerned.

What I've found interesting during lockdown is how lots of people say 'good morning'. We have been more open to talking about what is important to us. I hope we take a step forward. I think this moment in history could see us negotiate a new, more peaceful way to live on this land. We can't undo the past, but we can change how we make sense of it. The challenge is for us to see ourselves differently in the world.

Audrey Fernandes-Satar is sixty-seven years old and lives in Fremantle. Audrey shared her story with Emily Joyce.

'It would not be an honest account of my life unless I shared my challenges. The challenges one faces over a lifetime are what help to build resilience for when you need it the most.'

Dot Hoffman

I live on my own because my husband Errol died of cancer over a year ago. I am still getting used to it. The loneliness has made me angry. It is a quiet anger, and it's frustrating too because that makes me feel ungrateful when, really, I've had a wonderful life. The coronavirus has made it worse. Throughout my life, I have been surrounded by people and now Errol is gone and I am alone with just Mia, my beautiful cat, for company. For me, resilience means recognising the need to allow time for grieving and to look for solutions to the loss. This has been hard with COVID-19, because so many of the solutions for me are actually about spending time with people.

The isolation created by lockdown means I don't feel useful anymore. My great-grandchild, Evelyn, is who I have really missed. She is five now and both her parents work. From when she was first born, Errol and I were needed and, really, we've helped raise her. I have always felt that the fullness of life comes from being helpful and I wish people could understand that.

Some days I have a good cry, and I say to God, *Please forgive me for feeling so lonely because I know you're here and I am not really alone.*

I was born on a kitchen bench in 1943, four years after Adolf Hitler invaded Poland. My mother, Susanna, was a kind-hearted nurse with a gift for numbers. Throughout the war she was stationed at a Red Cross hospital in the city of Lahr, 13 kilometres from the border with France. My father was an engineer who had joined the air force as an apprentice. But on the occasion of my birth? His job was as a midwife. My mother had pursued Willi Ihlenfeld, my father, on a train from Berlin to Freiberg. Intrigued to see a young man purchasing bananas rather than cigarettes, she followed him from the platform to his carriage and married him two years later. She was twenty-nine years old and he was three years younger. My mother was ahead of her time.

My parents were almost entirely apart in the early years of their marriage. Yet, as is the way, they still managed to find opportunities to conceive both myself and my older brother Peter. Not unlike today, neither parent could be at home to raise us so when Peter and I were born, we were promptly handed over to my very capable grandfather, Jacob Winter. When the war started, Jacob, his second wife and my three aunts moved to the family farm in the village of Nussloch, near Heidelberg. There, we were surrounded by friends and cousins. The three-story eighteenth-century stone farmhouse was on a large piece of land with an enormous barn. Over the decades the village had grown up around the grand old home. It had two exterior staircases, approximately fifteen bedrooms and at least two kitchens. Throughout the war we lived off the land, growing vegetables and tending to chickens and geese, and every year we would fatten and slaughter a pig. One of my jobs was to feed the rabbits.

My parents were far away, but they knew I was in excellent care. For my part, I felt loved and cared for in Nussloch, especially by my grandfather. He would take me on walks and, over time, taught me the names of the walnut and beech trees and how to count them. I still love walking today and during the coronavirus lockdown I often go for long walks, even on wet days when I need a raincoat and umbrella. I follow a creek, marvelling at the trees and changing seasons. My husband Errol loved walking too and in semi-retirement we moved onto five acres in the Grampians. Today, my daily walks are meditative, reminding me of life in Nussloch and my time with Errol.

I was so young during the war. I remember only the big things, such as my mother coming by train to visit on weekends. I recall being confined to a hospital bed in Heidelberg with pleurisy when I was two and a half. My only visitor was my grandfather and when the building was bombed, my fear was not the bombs but that he might never find me in the hospital's underground shelter. When the war ended, there was so much excitement at the return of the men. We were encouraged to line the roads to welcome them home. I was about five years old when the men stepped out of the tram. Standing at the front gate, all I saw were skeletons. The men were so gaunt they needed assistance to walk.

I was told my father would be on one of those trams and I prayed he wouldn't look like a skeleton. My prayers were answered because Papa bounded off the tram fit as a fiddle. This was because after hostilities ended in September 1945, my father had been transported to France. As a prisoner of war, he was put to work on a farm but he did not live in hardship. He was fed well and even played soccer. Relieved and excited to see him healthy and to have him home, I took to him immediately, while my brother Peter was more cautious. We later discovered my father had been shot down twice during his time in active service and, on the second occasion, was very badly injured. He was rescued and taken to a makeshift hospital. He was discharged and cared for by a local family, with whom he spent the best part of a year recuperating, before returning to active duty.

My parents struggled to understand how Hitler was able to do what he did. By that stage, my mother had stopped nursing and was working in the village helping refugees find work and accommodation. My mother was a very special person. She knew how to really listen, to be silent when someone is communicating their fears, and to treat people honestly and generously. At night there were many adult discussions about the need to leave our homeland and whether we should choose Canada, Argentina or Australia. I think my parents wanted to make a statement about the atrocities that had occurred during the war by leaving Germany. They ruled out Argentina because it was accepting Nazis and Canada because it was too cold.

I was eleven when we began the long journey to Melbourne. But first, we were isolated, COVID-19 style, in the German city of Hanau for about six weeks. We were confined to a two-bedroom apartment with only a small communal garden with fruit trees. It was to prevent the spread of deadly diseases like tuberculosis and pleurisy. My parents had missed so much of our childhood, however, that they relished the isolation. I remember Dad's enjoyment in teaching me to play chess. From there we went to Bremen and boarded a ship for the three-month journey to Port Melbourne.

In February 1954 we were transported to our new lives aboard the Norwegian-built ship, the *Skaubryn*. I was quite distressed at abandoning my grandfather. It is the first time I recall feeling this quiet anger, the one that sits with me now. I became withdrawn and I would search out quiet parts of the ship where I could read. I was a prolific reader of novels and history but I withdrew as a way of showing my mother I was grieving. When I'd farewelled my grandfather I had been too excited by the adventure of the trip to understand I would never see him again. So when we left Germany I was suddenly confused, sad and a bit angry. Eventually my mother twigged and helped me to understand that he would be well taken care of and I snapped out of it and enjoyed the facilities, especially the pool.

Our family arrived at Port Melbourne in mid-May and stayed on the boat until we were allowed to disembark the following day. From there, we were transported to the migrant centre at Bonegilla, near Albury. My first impressions of Australia were of delicious creamy Peters Ice Cream and prickly army blankets. Unlike many other migrants, Peter and I had been taught English, which meant our parents allowed us to skip lessons and we had a lovely time exploring the beautiful bush surrounds. Peter was the creative one and I was into learning. But we were the best of friends and while the other children went to school, we enjoyed each other's company.

Australia accepted a large number of migrants at this time, and so we were among many different nationalities. I'm not sure a lot of thought went into housing us all together though, because we were taunted about the war by children from opposing countries. There was one girl who would stand at the gate yelling, 'You murdered the Russians.' But still, what I remember most is our family being together and the little things, like Mum washing the dishes. We would all pitch in and help and we would sing. We would always sing. My love of music is from my mother, who could sing alto. In the village in Germany we would go to church and afterwards Mum and Dad would take us for a walk in the forest to a little pub for apple cider. They would hold hands and we would all sing, Mum in alto and Dad, well, he would sing and try to make us laugh. My second daughter has inherited my mum's voice.

At age seventeen, I met Errol Hoffmann through a Lutheran youth group and, as I often reminded him, whenever there was a dance he would always choose me. Our relationship was formalised on a car ride. Of course, my brother was in the back seat and Errol was driving. Instead of dropping us at the train station, he insisted on taking me all the way to our door. That was it, really. We were committed Christians and, of course, we believed that in order to have a sexual relationship we should marry. Errol supported me in going back to school to matriculate and eventually to university. We were academically minded, so it was important to us both.

The night before our wedding, my mother sat me down and said, 'Don't expect too much' – which I took to mean I shouldn't have high expectations of my wedding night. Errol and I vowed not to have sex before marriage, which we found really hard. There was a lot of kissing and some creeping hands but we took our vows seriously. We were married at Saint John's Lutheran Church in February 1963. Errol's youngest sister and a girl I met on the boat were my two bridesmaids. I think Mum knew the day would be challenging and I would have to be polite and meet a lot of new people. She was right; it was exhausting. Errol and I were both so tired by the end that we just cuddled and said to each other, *This is silly, let's wait to make love.* The next day we drove to Sydney on our honeymoon. It was a magical time. Most of our days were spent walking and holding hands. That never changed.

Errol was dedicated to his education and completed a PhD at Melbourne University, after which he was immediately promoted to lecturer. Errol was a mechanical engineer and spent his life researching and lecturing at Melbourne University. Over the course of his career, he published 146 academic papers on the safety of everything from seatbelts to road signs, making him one of the world's leading experts in ergonomics. I always shared a great interest in his work and the study is still filled with his papers. We had two daughters together, Anne and Kathryn, and a son, Robert. After giving birth to the children, I went back to study and eventually graduated with qualifications in social work following the completion of an arts degree. In a sense, it was my turn to study. I asked God to help find me a vocation where, like my mother, I could help people. Guess what? I went on to work for twenty-four years as a social worker.

Our lives were mostly filled with joy. We travelled a lot and even returned to my village to see the farmhouse painted in a whitewash with beautiful roses. It had become a home to overseas students. I now have six grandchildren and one great-grandchild. My father died at eighty but my mother lived until she was ninety-three, though unfortunately the last ten of those years with dementia. When she was in the nursing home, Errol would amuse himself by testing her arithmetic because even when everything else failed, her gift for numbers remained. Right to the end. I had a teacher in Germany who fostered my love of history and botany. But my mother was the person who created the opportunity for me to get a university education by looking after my kids when they were young and reassuring me that the kids weren't missing out by me being away from home. She had not been able to continue her career and wanted to make sure I got that chance. She told me what I needed to be told at exactly the right time.

I never took our good fortune for granted. Errol's father died at fifty-two years of age and so we decided to retire at fifty-five and sixty. We bought just over two hectares in the country and a beautiful home with a driveway lined with red gums. Errol and I both drew our inspiration from the mountains and the trees and helped out at the church. Errol suffered his first heart attack while we were living there and had to be flown to Melbourne. When he suffered a second heart attack, we knew it was time to start planning to move back to our Melbourne home, the one I now share with my cat, Mia. Errol did not die from a heart condition but from bowel cancer. I started my story by saying I am angry at losing Errol and that I am also fearful of losing my independence and my usefulness. I say this because it would not be an honest account of my life unless I shared my challenges. The challenges one faces over a lifetime are what help to build resilience for when you need it the most.

It is a challenge to live alone. At times I worry about the big issues facing young people. Global warming is possibly the biggest. I hope they will get through, but like them, I feel sorrow and frustration about Australian politics and the politicians' unwillingness to take action. COVID-19 is bringing a lot of unemployment for young people, but this will pass with time. I don't know what to say to them. Sometimes I struggle to find the right words and I have to find the patience to rely on other people to guess what I am trying to say. My daughter has convinced me to talk to a doctor but these things exacerbate my quiet anger. I know it will subside, and when it does, I will probably get to cleaning out Errol's study.

Dot Hoffman is seventy-seven years old and lives in Melbourne. Dot shared her story with Helen McCabe.

'Resilience is the ability to fall down eight times and get up nine. It is to get hit on the shoulder by a bouncer and not rub the spot that hurts. To be able to grasp life as a precious gift, even when it dashes your dreams.'

Catherine McGregor

This quote is attributed to Albert Einstein: 'There are two ways to live your life. One is as though nothing is a miracle. The other is as though everything is a miracle.' In this ephemeral age of desk-calendar wisdom and exhibitionist charlatans masquerading as 'influencers', I cannot be sure of the provenance of that pearl. But I can attest to its truth, and to its enduring veracity and applicability to my own life.

I should never have lived to see the twentieth century. I am an alcoholic and a drug addict. I took my last drink on 2 June 1990 and I have not tasted alcohol nor used an unprescribed drug since that night. The small group of hardcore drunks who used to occupy the stools at the Kauri Hotel opposite Blackwattle Bay in Sydney are all long dead. They watched me walk unsteadily to the door without a word of farewell, leaving a portion of that final schooner unfinished on the bar. As I departed, the familiar soundtrack to my Saturday evenings, the Sky Channel greyhound call, receded behind me. I never set foot in my favourite haunt again. Little did I know that I was leaving behind more than a pub: I was leaving behind a way of life that only those who have grappled with addictions can know.

As I write this it is mere days from the thirtieth anniversary of that Saturday evening. That I am even alive is miraculous and I have no rational explanation for that. That I am both alive and not drinking is beyond calculation, going by the odds of those now-deceased punters who occupied the bar stools around me. That I am alive in 2020, suspended between my sixty-fourth birthday and the thirtieth anniversary of abstaining from alcohol and living as a female transsexual, would confound even Albert Einstein.

If you are as scornful of the numinous as I was in 1990, then I will not argue with you. But I believe that I am sober and alive today through the grace of God. For thirty years I have been protected, I have been directed. I have been corrected. The central, abiding truth around which my life has come to be organised is my faith in the unseen and the unprovable. As the years elapsed, I concluded that I had quit drinking because of what alcohol had done *to* me. Then I came to a recognition of what it did *for* me. For a shy kid who lost a parent two days before Christmas in 1964, it gave me a sense of being part of the gang. One of the boys. As a transsexual, to whom the final onset of gender dysphoria took me to the brink of suicide, alcohol was a near mystical elixir. Despite being bright and an exceptional cricketer, I was sure men would discern effeminacy and softness in me. I was painfully shy. Gentle. A loner.

I entered the Royal Military College in 1974 in the wake of the Vietnam War when it was a spartan institution whose purpose was to produce young officers to fight wars. It gave me unfettered access to alcohol and at last I felt I was a man among men. I thrived. My introversion dissolved in beer and I earned a reputation for reckless courage and disregard for my own physical safety. But the magic did not last long. Lapses in behaviour marred my stellar reputation. I topped my class in the first three years but was overlooked for the Sword of Honour on account of a growing cloud over my conduct when drunk.

Now, at age sixty-four, many things that animated my subconscious have come to the surface. I realise I should probably have transitioned gender at around the age of twenty-five. By then, my curiosity about transsexuals had become more of an obsession. I had furtively sought out some of the showgirls from Les Girls while in Sydney on sporting trips. I was aghast when carousing army mates arrived at the same venue, and I lamely made excuses before shamefully fleeing into the night lest they know why I was really there.

Both my devotion to my darling mother and my deeply inculcated, unconscious fear of eternal damnation forced me to deny my feelings. Sure, those showgirls were gorgeous, and they had lived as men for a time. But I was not like them . . . surely not? Like my father and his father, I was a soldier. I was admired by men and at ease among them. I played serious rugby and cricket. Living as a woman with that affected falsetto voice and ribald humour about tucking away the tackle? No way. I would rather die. And I nearly did.

I became a daily drunk. For most of the final three years of my drinking I never drew a sober breath. It was a squalid, painful half-life. Behind the bawdy banter and the inebriated abandonment, behind the loss of inhibition, lay a darker reality.

Mornings. I was usually violently ill upon awakening (not that you would flatter the self-induced coma that I entered at around 3 or 4 am with the description of 'sleep'). If I passed out in the house that I was sharing with a benevolent friend, that was some consolation. Occasionally I awoke in a police cell, having been found asleep on the footpath, or taken there by a cab driver who could exact neither payment nor a coherent address from me.

Mornings. They brought the inevitable onset of the shaking and sweating. I'd lose the futile battle against my rising gorge and vomit into the toilet bowl. Time for another drink, preferably Scotch, to settle the tremors and hyperventilation. I usually arrived at work drunk or else trembling violently. I never quite mastered drinking just enough to control the shaking without also slurring my words. I was dying. I rarely ate food. Almost never, frankly. But I also experienced frequent blackouts where slabs of time were erased from memory. *Have I really done what they told me I did?*

The morning after I left the pub for the final time, I awaited the onset of the terrors and physical symptoms. I was a militant atheist in constant rebellion against my very strict Catholic upbringing. And yet, I prayed aloud. A holy man whom I admire says that the only true prayers come from the broken-hearted. In the Garden of Gethsemane, in the face of gruesome death and having been betrayed by his most trusted friends, Jesus pleaded that he be spared. Then he simply surrendered to the inevitable, 'Thy will not mine be done.'

I was neither that eloquent nor that compliant on that Sunday morning. I bargained, 'Please God. Let me live. I am dying. Just don't let me die and I will stop drinking.' That, from a terrified atheist whose confidence in his intellect would make

Malcolm Turnbull seem as humble as the Dalai Lama. Call me delusional. Tell me that I made a decision. Tell me I just pulled up my socks and got on with it. You are entitled to your opinion. But it happened to me. Thirty years on I consider that it was a radical conversion experience.

With a history of seizures and hallucinations I should have been hospitalised and probably tapered off substances with Valium. But I have never found a sedative that I did not like to chew like Smarties. So, I detoxified without formal support. No seizures. No cravings. I even ate food – off a plate. My desperate prayer had been answered. Yet even despite that, I continued to sneer at belief and to resist the concept of God. But slowly, as the fog of alcohol dissipated, I realised that something beyond mere mortal comprehension was happening inside me.

If alcoholic drinking was a slow-motion form of self-harm, I never once contemplated ending my own life during my active drinking escapades. Rather, I have only contemplated suicide since I quit drinking, and for that I have no medical or psychiatric explanation. I can only speculate, based on what my life has felt like over the past three decades. Without sedating chemicals or alcohol, life in its raw form has often felt intolerably painful. More than once I have wanted to enter deep sleep and not awaken to another day. But I trudge on, sustained by faith. Aeschylus warned before Jesus was even born, 'Man must suffer. Suffer unto truth.'

Mine is merely a story of survival. Ultimately, every human life that ebbs away to its natural conclusion is that. As a believer, I accept that this world is a vale of tears. No one is spared loss; all experience sickness, bereavement and failure. All of us are on our way to the final destination to navigate that Boulevard of Broken Dreams. So, as the twilight gathers and the grave beckons, I cannot share any exemplary secrets for those struggling to survive. Sure, my life has been a struggle. Then again, so have those of millions of others who share this fleeting moment in eternity on this fragile little planet with me. I am unpersuaded that there is anything remarkable about my survival nor that I possess more resilience than billions who cling to daily existence amid squalor, poverty, war and disease.

My erratic emotions and internal torture are very much First World problems, though I had made a decision long before gender transition that I wanted to make a life rather than make a living. Accordingly, the most female characteristic I possess is the absence of retirement savings. The prospect of growing old alone and in poverty is real and now assuming a degree of inevitability. The recent collapse of the economy effectively ended my plans of working for as long as my health permitted. My craft is words, and media work has evaporated. Well into my seventh decade, the words of Shakespeare's Richard II both haunt and rebuke me for my feckless decisions: 'I wasted time and now doth time waste me.'

Why did I keep climbing the mountain when the journey seemed futile? Why did I live on in a body for so long that was at war with a mind, incessantly demanding the radical transformation to a decent life? Why did I destroy a happy marriage and leave a beautiful home? Why did I disrupt my family and bewilder my friends? Maybe, as the religious zealots insisted, I was delusional. Insane. Beguiled by Satan into blindness to my own depravity. Perhaps this is still true.

In the end, I suppose I simply chose life over death. No matter the cost, I decided that I would live as some version of a woman. Anyone who has felt dysphoric knows that the choice in the end is that simple. The torment is beyond words. It is relentless and simply will not abate. More than once since the sudden resurgence of my intense feelings of gender incongruity, in November 2011, I have had to summon every ounce of resolve merely to refrain from self-extinction. I chose to run the gauntlet of ridicule, rejection and contempt in choosing to live the final portion of my life as a transsexual. In pursuing survival, I found myself. But I also lost many things of great value. Not a day passes without regret.

I weep for the loss of the love of my life. I weep for the annihilation of the little blond boy so dearly loved by his wonderful parents. The list is long. But to the zealots I assert that I am at peace with one thing and it is this: I am living my life in alignment with the will of loving God. I shall live with eternal judgement. I have neither the time nor the energy to masquerade as a guru of positive thinking or the triumph of willpower over adversity. I am alive through the grace of God. In my darkest hours I continued to pray. I clung to life when it made no sense at all. I drew comfort from the simple beauty of the Gospel of Matthew, that if God so cares for the birds of the air and the lilies of the field, will he surely not care for me?

As an American pastor whose preaching I admire, says, 'If you have pulse, then you have purpose. Every man, every woman, every animal, every bird, every plant has been created by design.'

When you contemplate the odds of breaking that invisible membrane between non-existence and fragile, vulnerable human life, then every single one of us is a miracle. Life is a precious gift not to be thrown away wantonly no matter how painful it has become. Or at least so I believe.

So why believe? When I slowly, and reluctantly, became aware that something outside my rational mind and beyond my own limited consciousness had relieved my obsession with alcohol and drugs, I gradually began to awaken to a divine presence that I call God. Could I debate with Richard Dawkins and convince him or an audience that God exists? Probably not. But I am alive – and that is in spite of my own worst instincts.

Two times when I had both the means and inclination to end my life, people inexplicably intervened. On Christmas night, 1992, I was sitting on my balcony on the eighteenth floor of a Gold Coast hotel, inhaling deeply and trying to muster the courage to jump. The phone rang. I answered it. I chatted to my friend with the noose still around my neck. Gender dysphoria had driven me to that awful place. Yet my deep commitment to not drinking denied me even the comfort of a bottle of Scotch to fortify my resolve. I survived and repressed my gender conflicts for another two decades.

On Australia Day 2012 I had accumulated over 200 sleeping tablets. Again, I was torn about dying intoxicated after so long sober. But I choose to believe that again the invisible hand of God placed a person in my path to puncture the neurosis engulfing my teeming brain. I had shot a scene for a film about cricket outside the Adelaide Oval and my mates insisted that I join them for dinner. We laughed at the absurdity of life on the road and I went back to my lonely room and flushed my pills down the cistern. It was the last time I had both the means and the intent to end my life, though I have flirted with ending my anguish at intervals since. But I pray and draw nourishment from a small group of deep friends.

Resilience is the ability to fall down eight times and get up nine. It is to get hit on the shoulder by a bouncer and not rub the spot that hurts. To be able to grasp life as a precious gift, even when it dashes your dreams. I love poetry in particular. The final word belongs to my favourite poet, Robert Frost, who told of 'two roads diverged in a yellow wood' and taking the one 'less travelled by' – and that making all the difference . . . I do not know what the future holds, but I believe I know who holds the future. And I am grateful for the gift of life.

Catherine McGregor is sixty-four years old and lives in Canberra. As told by Catherine McGregor, speaking for herself.

'Nowadays I get very upset with people complaining about meaningless things. I think to myself, At least you still have food. You still have a home. You don't have any problems. *The truth is that all of us need to learn to be resilient.'*

Jutta Dowdy

When the Allies bombed our house in August 1943, we were hiding in the cellar. I recall the sirens going off while the Allied planes were overhead dropping bombs. The noise above us as the house collapsed around us was almost indescribable. It was deafening. The sound was so loud that even today, I hate loud noises. I still scream in a thunderstorm. The cellar smelled like wet cement, and I can't stand that smell anymore either. I was nearly seven years old when it happened. Hamburg was flattened and nearly 50,000 people died.

My Uncle Hermann came with a trailer to get us out, which was difficult because of the rubble. There were burned bodies everywhere. The sky was blood red and glowing. Parachutes with men dangling from them were slowly descending to earth. God only knows where they landed in that inferno. The air was thick with haze and smoke and we couldn't breathe properly. My mum grabbed a large zinc container full of wet laundry and we held items of soggy clothing to our faces. We had to make a lot of detours in order to get to safety. Uncle Hermann took us to Bergedorf, about 18 kilometres from Hamburg, to live with Grandma. Though Hamburg had been destroyed, this place nearby where the rest of the family lived was almost untouched.

Dad was mainly away at war when I was young but when he was home, I was his favourite. He did spoil me. There were the three older children and the two little ones, and I was the second-last child. Dad came from a wealthy family; he was the only surviving child of a successful import and export merchant. Dad's sibling, a girl, died from rheumatoid arthritis at the age of thirty-one. I was named after her. Dad had some luxuries early on in his life. He had French and English govern-esses and therefore became fluent in both these languages. My grandfather took him to the London Stock Exchange at a very early age to teach him all the ins and outs of business. It was practical learning.

My grandfather lost everything in the stock market crash of 1928–29. He lost millions of dollars, and his factories in Calcutta, India. His stocks became worthless. I remember using the individually issued share certificates to draw pictures on. My father's mother had died and my grandfather then married her sister. Life changed drastically for the whole family after that. My grandfather's new wife was always jealous of her sister for having a big beautiful house. Instead of putting the money left in my grandfather's will towards us children's education, she spent it on herself. My grandfather had wanted us to go to a fancy school in Switzerland but after he died, that never came to be.

We stayed with my mother's mother, my grandma, for a while after the bombings but it was too hard for her to have six extra people in the house. One of my aunts said to her, 'Well, you are not an asylum for homeless people.' We had to go elsewhere. That somewhere was Nakel near Bromberg, Poland, which was occupied by Germany at the time. This was quite a pleasant period in my life, despite the ongoing war. The landscape was beautiful. There were stork nests on the roofs. We would go for walks along a cherry-tree-lined avenue to go swimming in the river Netze. We'd go hunting for crayfish at night with a torch. We had enough food to eat there and we even had a dog, a little terrier.

This relatively good life in Poland came to an abrupt end in January 1945, when the Russians arrived. They came in from the East. My brother Uwe packed madly. We had this beautiful big washing basket and he was throwing everything into it. I can still see him dropping my doll headfirst into the basket. We left in the early hours of the morning. I had my pyjamas on as I had been in bed sick with cystitis, an inflammation of the bladder. We could hear the gunfire of Russians coming closer and a German government contact told my mother to get out fast. Everything was left behind. My mother took only a suitcase each of flour and sugar, and a metal box with all the family history in it. That metal box, with the family's identification documents, was important. You were always having to prove you weren't Jewish.

Nowadays I get very upset with people complaining about meaningless things. I think to myself, *At least you still have food. You still have a home. You don't have any problems.* The truth is that all of us need to learn to be resilient, and resilience means not giving up. To keep going. I believe that when you're busy you don't get down on yourself and think about depressing things. You don't analyse them too much. You don't sit down and think, *Gee, am I resilient? Can I go on?* Keeping busy and keeping going is very important in that way.

It was deep winter in January 1945 when we boarded the last passenger train to leave Nakel. Dad was a prisoner in Siberia, so he wasn't with us. Hundreds of people left on the station platform were exposed to the Russians. I knew one girl and I remember her standing there with her mother. I wondered what would happen to her. Our family was lucky to have a whole compartment to ourselves but, unfortunately, this did not last. No sooner had we left the station than there was a huge crash. Our train had collided with another steam engine. It was a huge shock. The suitcase with flour came crashing down from the overhead rack and the flour entirely covered my brother. He looked like a snowman. It would have been funny if my mother had not been so worried by the loss of the precious foodstuffs, which were supposed to feed us, and also wondering how we would get away now.

We had to get out of that train and were herded into a cattle train with more than sixty people in each wagon, sitting and lying on sacks. A potty was handed around for people to relieve themselves. The idea of doing your business in front of strangers was intimidating. When the train stopped at some point, we were told: 'If you want to, you can jump out and do your business in the snow.' Those events are so vivid for me, even now. I can see myself outside, beside the train and sitting in the snow, peeing. I have my little brown coat on. The fear that the train would leave without me is still palpable. We still had the suitcase of sugar and another passenger had some tea. So, we melted the snow and made sweet tea to drink while we travelled.

Though it was not a very long distance to Hamburg, the cattle train still took three days and nights. This was how we found out the cattle train was heading to Berlin. When my mother realised this, she made a quick but very wise decision. She wanted to go back to Bergedorf, where her family was, so instead of staying on the train, which would eventually end up in the East Sector, she realised we had to get off. She took me and my sister by the hand and we jumped off the moving train when entering Berlin station, while my brother followed with the box full of our family history. Everything else we left behind.

It's strange to think of my mother at that time. She was born in 1899, so she was only in her forties when all this happened, which is half my current age. She was trying to survive by herself in a war with all her kids. She was a smart person and so brave.

In Berlin, we stayed overnight in a huge bunker, where we received a meal. Then we found a train to take us to Bergedorf. The only one available was an army passenger train. It had lots of tired soldiers in each compartment and I was allowed to sit on the lap of one of them.

We lived in Bergedorf for a long time after escaping Poland. My father was absent during the war years, like so many men in those days. Sometimes he was granted leave to come home for Christmas, but then he was called away again within an hour. So we saw very little of him.

For a few years, things returned to normal, except that we were so cold and hungry. We mainly stayed in bed and covered up to keep warm. We really were starving. Little kids like us would go to the countryside to ask for food. Either you got the dogs set onto you or perhaps, if you found someone kind, they might give you some apples. Otherwise you could pick some weeds and eat them. Often the police came and took the food you'd scavenged. They were hungry too, of course. Many of the local schools had been used as hospitals by the army. We had to walk miles and miles through the snow to get to school, and didn't have proper footwear. If it hadn't been for my mother, I probably would have lost all my toes from frostbite. Treating them daily with ointment and bandages saved them.

Right before the end of the war in 1945, the British army crossed the River Elbe into Bergedorf. Some idiot Germans started shooting at them and of course they retaliated. The adults knew trouble was brewing, but as kids we had no idea. My grandmother had told us not to leave the backyard when playing, but we didn't do what we were told and we all left the backyard during our games. Had we stayed, I probably wouldn't be sitting here today. Grenades were flying all around and damaged the back wall of the house and garden. I remember running across the road, trying to get home while the grenades were whistling around my head. I could not push open the front door. It was an eerie feeling because there was this weird pressure in the air. I don't know the physics of it, maybe it came from the bombings. I also remember the feeling of intense fear. When I did manage to get into the house, someone opened the door to the cellar, where everyone else had already assembled to hide from the British army. Later, when things calmed down, we discovered forty-five people had been killed.

After the initial standoff between the British soldiers and us, the fighting stopped. We were given chocolate by the soldiers. We invited them into our homes, and they enjoyed that, especially my grandmother's cooking. War is strange like that.

In 1948 my father returned home. The Russians released him because of an open wound in his leg. Like many returning soldiers, he found it hard to adjust and to care for a family. It was difficult for him to find work. Eventually, my dad left our family for another woman. To be honest, we hadn't seen him for so long that it didn't really have much impact on us. At that stage, the three youngest children were still at home with Mum and had to be supported. I had to leave school before I turned fifteen because I needed to earn money and help with the household. I cried for days. I desperately wanted to continue my education.

I got an apprenticeship in a wholesale chemical company and completed a business diploma. That course trained you from top to bottom on how a company runs. I stayed there working in Hamburg until I was nearly twenty. But by then, I wanted an adventure. At school I was always looking at the globe and wanted to go somewhere exciting, either to Canada or Sweden as an au pair. My older sister and brother-in-law and their young son had already been living in Australia for a year, so my mother felt it would be a better idea if I went there. I took the trip by boat to Australia, which lasted thirty days. My sister met me in Melbourne harbour. The family lived in Port Fairy near Warrnambool. I remember drives on the Great Ocean Road showing me the beautiful ocean views.

Next, I had my first journey by plane, flying up to Canberra where an aunt and her family lived. One of my cousins was working at Reid House, which was one of many government hostels. I had just started working in the dining room, collecting plates, etc., and had only been there for a few hours when the boss came to me and said, 'I believe you know about business.'

And I said, 'Yes.' I ended up in the office right away, which was wonderful. I ran the office there, making bookings for government employees and that kind of thing. The hostel housed approximately 300 guests, mainly workers from the Snowy Mountains Scheme. I was charged with the daily office work and only had to answer to the manager and his wife, who were running the place. And that's where I met my husband.

I booked the man who I eventually married into the hostel after his return from Germany. He was very attractive and we just clicked. When I met him, I was saving to go back to Germany. He knew I wanted to go home and so he got me pregnant, which was very calculated and made my decision very hard. Even now, I wish I'd had the guts to leave him and return home, despite expecting a baby. Instead, I stayed with him in a not very favourable marriage. We had four daughters: Karen, Helen, Irene and Ingrid, and always our own home. My husband worked at the University of New South Wales, then the University of New England and, at the end, at the University of Queensland.

Being in a foreign country without family support was very difficult. So I stayed in the marriage. Honestly, looking back, I wish I hadn't. I was not able to study, as I had to look after four children, the house and the garden. Women are permitted to be far more independent now. Women can work and be married at the same time. I had no help from my husband, and I was often exhausted. He read and collected his books. Instead of being an example to the children, he would demand rather than ask.

During annual sabbatical visits to Germany, my children were able to enjoy being among the extended family. My husband's many affairs should have given me rise to leave my marriage, especially while we were living in Germany. I should never have returned to Australia after another of these affairs, but where would I have lived with four children? That was fifty years ago. If you gave me the chance now, I'd be out the door like a rocket.

I only came into my own and discarded the emotional intimidation when I went back to work in 1979 and gained control over my finances. That's a lesson for all young women: You need to be financially independent. Never rely on a man to house and support you. I was over forty by then and my youngest child was nine years old. I was offered a position by a German company that was building large excavators for the coal industry. I ran that office and often got to speak German again, which was wonderful. It was a million-dollar company and I was frequently left in charge when the director went overseas or on holiday. I did it well. That's when I started keeping my money separate. I would always suggest that women keep their accounts separate.

By far the biggest tragedy of my life is my second daughter, Helen, who died by suicide on 31 May 1994. You never get over something like that. When I found out, I thought my whole insides were going to be pulled out of me. It is just the most horrible thing. Helen was a vibrant, intelligent and beautiful personality. She was a wonderful amateur actress and maybe because of that she was able to hide her feelings. I can still see her in my mind. I suppose I can never really know what happened and why. I do know that Helen lost her home due to a failed business venture. Her boys were nine and eleven when she took her life and that, I just can't understand. I suppose it shows how desperate she must have felt. Helen loved the boys so much. They will never get over her death.

I still think about the morning when the dreaded phone call came to tell me that Helen was dead. I knew my daughter was psychologically vulnerable. She had been seeing a psychologist before she died. It was raining and miserable outside that day. I kept thinking to myself that I should ring Helen's husband and tell him to not let her out of his sight. But being at work and for whatever reason, I didn't call.

The way I survived was by doing the martial art aikido. The emphasis on mind and body coordination helped me to get on with life. It gave me inner strength. I met so many wonderful people through that activity. It saved me.

My husband died two years ago, right in front of me. I'd been nursing him for over a year when he succumbed to dementia and lost the use of his legs. I'd get woken up at night due to his many falls. Every little fall meant he would bleed because he was on blood thinners, so I was always washing his bed-clothes. It was exhausting. When he died, of course, in those first moments it was a shock but then it was a bit of a relief. I am quite happy with my own company now. I'm not running out to meet Mr Right at a dance club! And if my husband came back now? Well, I would not make the same mistake in marrying him, although I am thankful for the children, grandchildren and great-grandchildren. Hopefully they will be resilient and get ahead in life.

Jutta Dowdy is eighty-four years old and lives in Brisbane. Jutta shared her story with Ginger Gorman and Emily Joyce.

'Only love can change things. Hate can't do anything in the face of love. This means that sometimes you must find a way to forgive even the worst things. I am a Buddhist and so I believe in karma . . . I tell young people to be kind and to live in peace.'

Be Ha

I was born in an auspicious year: 1950, the Year of the Tiger. Our family moved to Sa Dec, a town near the Mekong River Delta, when I was five years old. We lived there until 1975 when the Communists came to Vietnam. I am the oldest in a very big family. I have eleven brothers and sisters. My life was happy as a child and, most of all, I loved to eat. Especially chicken rice. To make this, they used a chicken broth to boil the rice in, so it tasted delicious. Then they would chop the chicken into pieces, and you could dip it in the fish sauce and ginger. Oh so yummy.

My father used to buy spare auto parts in Saigon for his garage business, and I remember that one day he wanted to take me with him. I was so happy – it was the first time I had been to the big city and I was especially excited to go with my father. How busy it was on the streets in Saigon. Oh my goodness! I stopped and looked at everything, everywhere. My father had to hurry me along. I said 'wow' because I was a country girl going to the big city and it was unbelievable to me. When my father arranged for us to stay in a hotel, at night-time I looked out the window and was dizzied by the big buildings, and even the cinema.

I have loved cooking since I was ten years old and vividly remember the day when my father took me to a nice restaurant for the first time. Oh, the dishes that I ate that day! My father had lots of business meetings at that restaurant because the owner was his close friend. The owner let me go out to the kitchen and watch the chef work. I did that until I was fourteen years old, always watching and learning. That is my most happy time and cooking became my hobby for life. I love it. I have an ambition to one day set up a cooking school here in Melbourne. Food is a part of culture and I want to share our Vietnamese culture with the world. We could also help unemployed people and low-income people by offering very low-cost meals to them. I would love to do it this way; not to make a profit but to serve the food to everyone who needs it.

I met my husband, Dien, when I was seventeen. At that time, he was a very good-looking but shy man. He is ten years older than me, which made my parents worried. Mum said that maybe he already had a wife back home! Dien was from central Vietnam, and I was from the south, so we had no way of checking his marital status. We had a relationship for more than two years. When I passed my high school exam, I won a scholarship to Japan to study but I decided I wouldn't go because it might upset my boyfriend. My parents were not happy about that – but I loved him.

My husband was so young when his father passed away. There was a group who did not like the French government and they did not like those people who worked for the French government. This group, who would later become the Vietcong, came to the village where my father-in-law and his family lived, and they shot my father-in-law. My mother-in-law died not long after that and so Dien was raised by his older brother. Dien missed his parents, but you must understand that in Vietnam, parents are very strict and fathers are not close to their children. They love them very much, of course, but fathers don't show much affection the way they do here. They do not hold their children so often or kiss them. Instead, they work hard to make a better future for their children. I think, for this reason, my husband was okay even after his parents died.

Here in Australia, parents feel they need to be their children's friend. That is not how we Vietnamese people do things. The Australian parents are so close to their young children growing up and know all their children's friends' names! Years later, when we lived in Australia, my husband and I could not do that, even though it was the culture here. We came to this country with nothing and we had to work many jobs, at night and on the weekends too. We did not have time for playing, or have lots of money to buy toys for the children. We had to start all over again after the Communists came to Vietnam and we were forced to leave our country.

It was in 1968, the Year of the Monkey, when the Communists came and took over Hue, the province where my husband lived. It happened over a week, and they killed a lot of Vietnamese people. Vietnamese soldiers fought to take back control over the town and they were victorious, so life returned to normal. But still, the Vietnamese military needed more soldiers. They needed more people because they knew the Communists would return.

At that time my husband Dien was a principal in a primary school but when the war became more serious, everyone had to join the Vietnamese army. Dien became a soldier.

My husband was a lieutenant in the army when we met. Some friends organised a dinner-dance party to help me celebrate my eighteenth birthday, without telling my parents, and Dien was invited. Back then, if the girls danced in the Western style with a partner it was very naughty. It was not what nice girls did. Someone told my mum and dad and my goodness! My father was so angry. He yelled at me and he did not talk to me for more than a week. Dien now says to me sometimes as a flirtatious joke, 'Do you want to have a dancing lesson again?'

In Vietnam, traditionally, if you are not married then you cannot go out together. And so Dien and I never had a chance to be together alone before we were married. My parents permitted him to visit me but only on the weekend, when they were present. One day he asked if he could take me to a movie and my mum said maybe, if I took my number six sister along with me. My mum told my sister that she had to sit in between us!

Dien and I were married in October 1969. I wore a traditional Vietnamese white dress. Our daughter Vu Lan was born in 1972, and my son Tri followed in 1973. Last year, when my husband and I celebrated our fiftieth wedding anniversary, my sister told our guests the story of her keeping us apart all that time ago.

The fall of Saigon happened six years after we were married, on 30 April 1975. We called it the Black April. Officers who had worked for the old regime, like my husband, were told to come to a camp and bring food with them for a few days. After that, it was expected they could go home again. Instead, the Communists took them to a kind of prison, which they called a re-education camp, and my husband was there for three years. I was so very sad when they took my husband away. I was still young and got so scared, especially at night. If someone knocked on our door after dark, I would not open it. I tried to keep myself occupied and busy. I said to the children that one day we would see their father again. I never let myself believe he would die at the re-education camp, though of course many people did.

When Saigon fell to the Communists, there was a big massacre in our city. The Communists killed lots of people in different ways; they burned them, and they pushed them into a hole. Days later, Communist soldiers came to my parents' house and store. They stayed there. They slept there. They took food from our fridge. They helped themselves to everything without asking us. They acted like it was their own house. They wrote down everything we had in the house and the store too. Then they demanded that my mum and dad sign papers, giving all their assets, houses and land to the Communists. They robbed us of all the belongings that my parents had been working very hard for all their lives. The Communists told my parents to leave their house. Mum was crying but she was not scared. She said, 'You cannot do this, you cannot steal from us.' Everything was gone. All gone.

After that, all the family came to my house to live with my children and me; my parents and all of my brothers and sisters. That meant fifteen people in one small house. We had nothing left. We had empty hands. My father loved the countryside very much and had owned a farm about 6 kilometres from my family house where we'd grown everything we needed. The Communists took that too, including the spot my father had wanted to be a family cemetery. The rules changed after the Communists came, as well. Households were given a certificate with a list of how many people lived there. The police could come to your house at any time to inspect the certificate and if someone was living there who should not be, they would go to jail. The Communists would calculate how much food we were entitled to eat in a month and that was all we could buy. A hundred grams of meat per day for all of us and only a little rice, fish sauce or salt and sugar.

Nearly one year later, I was allowed to go to the re-education camp and visit my husband. My children, especially my three-year-old son, wanted to come and he cried when I said he couldn't. I was scared about what he might see and worried that I would not be able to give him what he needed. It might be dangerous on the journey. My mother convinced me to take him because we really did not know what would happen to Dien; there was a chance my son might never see him again. It was a very long way, too far for a child. The journey was three or four hours by boat and then a long walk for 6 kilometres from the port. I could hardly carry all the things I had brought for Dien because it was so heavy, but I tried.

My husband looked different when I saw him. He was older and thinner. Dien had been doing hard labour and was only given rice and a small portion of vegetables to eat. No flavour. No meat. I brought some roast duck for Dien but when we got to the camp, my son was so hungry that he ate some of it. Dien boiled water from a small river for us to drink but I couldn't do it. I spat it away because it wasn't clean and tasted very sour. When I talked to my husband, there were officers around, so I couldn't say anything true. I only cried. A lot of his friends passed away there because of illness and because there was no treatment or medicine. We saw Dien only for a little while, then we had to go home. It was very hard.

The Communists released Dien after three years. I got a letter telling me to come and bring him home. I was so happy, so happy. On the first night after Dien arrived, he told me that the electric lights in our house were too bright for him. In the camp there had been no electricity at all. Only candles. His eyes were shocked by the light. Dien could not work anymore to support the family. Dien never dared tell anything about his life to a stranger because they might report him. He trusted no one. My children did not recognise their father because they were young when he left, and he had changed so much. Dien was smaller and his skin was much darker. He had always been shy but after having to keep his mouth shut in the re-education camp for so long, he became even more quiet. Sometimes I would see him sitting, looking into the somewhere. It was like he was not here.

Dien and I spoke to my parents, who said that if we stayed in Vietnam, there was no guarantee my husband wouldn't be taken away again. My husband was distantly related to the royal family, so we would be in danger always. We decided that we had to leave Vietnam for freedom and for my children's future. My mother sold her jewellery on the black market and gave us some money to pay for our escape. We paid five pieces of gold for each adult, and three pieces of gold for each child. I could not sleep the night before we left. In the middle of the night my mum woke up my little daughter. My mother spat into my daughter's hands so that she would never forget her.

I was sad to leave my parents and everyone I loved, but I knew that we had to go. We had to seek death to find life. I looked everywhere from the boat on the border of Vietnam. I looked around everywhere, trying to remember because I thought I may never see this – or them – ever again. I worked in the kitchen at a Melbourne nursing home for a while and sometimes would go to speak with the elderly people in their rooms. They would tell me how they were lonely and show me photos of their families but sometimes their children would never even come to visit them because they were working. Even though they lived very close! We have a different way in Vietnam. For Vietnamese people, you have a duty to your parents, always.

But still, I had no second thoughts about leaving my family because we would have been killed if we went back to the village. We were 150 people together in a small fishing boat that was only 12 metres long. We sat next to each other like sardines. We had packed food for only one week as there was no money to get more and no room to take it anyway. The journey became my nightmare. There were Thai pirates who attacked us. Twice. I was more frightened than I had ever been in my life and thought we might die. The first time they attacked, they took everything we had on the boat and destroyed the engine, but thankfully nobody was raped or killed. The second time was just a day later. Seven pirates boarded our boat and acted like animals. They took all our men onto their boat and kept the women and children on our boat. They separated us.

Our Vietnamese captain said to our men that they had to be strong and fight, otherwise we would all die and our bodies would be dumped in the sea. The married and old people were scared to fight because what if we died and the children were left all alone? Some of the young men without children did the fighting. They sacrificed their lives in order for us to survive.

The Thai pirates were few in number, but they had knives and swords. Everyone fought each other and four of our young men died. Our captain was killed. After the battle, we all slowly boarded the Thai pirates' empty boat. We brought our captain's body with us. The Thai pirates had some ice that was supposed to keep their fish fresh and we placed our captain's body on the ice to preserve it. I remember that I wept for him.

The elderly people told us again and again of the traditional ways. That is, wherever you die, you have to be buried. Otherwise, we believe, the spirit can become trapped on earth. Our captain had left behind two sons, including a little boy of maybe three years old. He was too young to understand. He knew his father was injured because there had been a lot of blood, but he did not know what death was. We tied a piece of white material around the two little boys' heads as a symbol of mourning. All of the children were asked to kneel down and we knelt beside them and prayed together. We found a piece of metal to tie to the captain's body, so it would not float, and we returned the captain's body to the sea.

Dust to dust. Sea to sea. I will never forget that moment.

We remained on the boat that had belonged to the Thai pirates, but we had no working engine and no captain. For a week, we just floated at sea. Many other boats passed by, but nobody would rescue us. In the morning it was very hot and at night it would get cold, so cold. I only had one t-shirt and one pair of pants because the pirates took everything else from us. I'd brought with me on the boat some cards that were sort of like tarot cards. I would take cards from my pocket and ask about our future. I never once picked up the card that said I would die or that a disaster would happen. Somehow, I knew we would be safe. I believed that we would reach land one day and have a new life.

We had almost nothing to eat. We had taken some of the Thai pirates' fish but among 150 people, it only made one meal. We started to run out of water. It was so bad that we even tried to drink the sea water. We were desperate. I always tried to talk to the elderly people to see how they were doing. Every day I would lie down at the front of the boat next to a very elderly man and talk to him. Then one morning I tried to wake him up and he did not answer. He had passed away because he was starving. We began to lose hope. It was so bad, I cannot even tell you. I cry to think of it.

Finally, our rescuers came. The wife of a doctor was doing her exercises on the deck of a British oil tanker named the *Entalina*. She told Captain Sloan, who was in charge of the oil tanker, and his crew to rescue us. There were big waves, so big. It was hard to bring the two boats together at sea. One minute they were close together and the next minute they were apart. Just as the British crew retrieved the last person from our boat onto their oil tanker, our boat disappeared in the waves. We could not have waited a moment longer. By that time, we had been lost for nearly twenty days on the ocean.

We were so smelly that the British used a hose to spray and wash us down. For many, many days we had been without a toilet. We went wee-wee over the side of the boat with no way to wash. I was twenty-nine years old and I still got a period. The smell was so bad. Once we were clean, we dried ourselves in the towels the people on the British oil tanker gave us. Then they dumped all of our towels in the sea. We had head lice, every one of us. The British chef gave us each one apple because we couldn't eat too much at once after being starving for so long. It was my first apple and it was so delicious. The next day we had a little porridge, slowly moving towards eating solid food again.

Soon we would arrive at the Port of Darwin. We were so happy. We knelt down to say thank you to our saviour Captain Sloan and the *Entalina* crew. Maybe Buddha looked after us but truly I do not know how we survived. My husband and I had family in America, but we had learned about Australia in school. We knew it had a small population, with a lot of land and a lot of farms – and the Australian people we met in Darwin were so friendly. We decided we wanted to stay. Our family has since travelled all around the world, but we know we made the right decision. The Australian people opened their arms and their hearts to welcome us. The first time I saw Melbourne at night-time I thought it was the most beautiful city. It had so much sky, and light.

Our family lived in a hostel in Melbourne for one year while we took English classes and found work. Dien got a job, first with the Holden car factory, and then later at a bakery in Clayton. I worked in a plastics factory while studying an interpreter course at RMIT in the evenings. My children went to Springvale Primary School, which is now called Springvale Rise Primary School. My children did find it hard because they are caught between two cultures. In Vietnam, children don't look in the eyes of an adult, they have to look down. One day at school I heard the principal yell at a child, 'Look at me.' I had to talk to him later and say, 'He is not allowed to look at your eyes, please. Please understand he has been taught that way.'

I worked at my children's primary school for twenty-four years as an administration assistant. I have only recently retired. I still volunteer for the Springvale Indochinese Mutual

Assistance Association and the Vietnamese Cultural Heritage Centre. I have tried to pay back the Australian community as best I can. My family did not come here to be a burden on the Australian people. I have been given an OAM and am a justice of the peace.

Some people still don't understand why my family is here in Australia. The first year I worked in the primary school, there were some people who didn't like us. They didn't say it but from their gestures and from the way they looked at me, I knew. What they don't understand is that nobody ever wants to leave their country and leave behind their loved ones. But sometimes you have to, for freedom. Through the years, my husband and I have worked hard, and I've done a lot of things to help people. Over time, those people became grateful for what I did for the school and that helped with the discrimination. They came to like me. Sometimes they would have international days at the school, for fundraising. I would cook spring rolls, fried rice, noodles, Vietnamese pancakes and more. Wow, the Australian people would even help do the cooking, and then, of course, help to eat it.

It was not always easy for me when the primary school would host its international days. Each classroom would have a country they'd dress up as and the little children would draw the flag of that country. I cannot accept the new Vietnamese flag. It is a Communist flag. I say now that I do not have a country anymore. The yellow flag with the three red stripes, the one I knew, is not the flag that is recognised now and that the children were told to draw. I wish they would put up two flags because our flag from before 1975 is part of Vietnamese history. But I understand it is too complicated for the Australian children. They do not know the politics.

Only love can change things. Hate can't do anything in the face of love. This means that sometimes you must find a way to forgive even the worst things. I am a Buddhist and so I believe in karma. Nobody is happy all their life and nobody suffers a sick, miserable life all of the time. If you do something cruel, then you will one day suffer again. I tell young people to be kind and to live in peace. I am lucky. I have a lovely family. It is not like that for everyone. I wish for the Australian people to know how lucky they are and to not waste their time here on earth. We only live one life. I will use the rest of mine well.

Be Ha OAM is seventy-one years old and lives in Melbourne. Be Ha shared her story with Jamila Rizvi.

'This isn't the first virus to be introduced into Australia. When the colonists came they brought influenza and thousands of our people died from the common flu because we'd never had it . . . We've had the coronavirus, but there will be another disease, and another, in time.'

Donna Meehan

It was during the winter of 1976 that I decided to end my life. Every winter I would have a bad winter. I always thought it was because I loved summer and the heat, but the more I work with Aboriginal people the more I understand that winter is a hard time for us – because we're locked indoors. Aboriginal people are outdoors people. We love the sunshine and the freedom it brings. I thought the only people who loved me were my husband and my adoptive parents. For a long time, I didn't feel worthy of that love because in my mind, I was fat and ugly and black. That was my distorted vision of myself. My son was four years old and I thought he'd be better off without me.

A child of the Stolen Generation, I hadn't found my family back then – and they hadn't come to find me. I was feeling lonely and displaced. At the very moment I decided to end my life, my son ran inside. He'd picked a little bunch of flowers from the garden and he came right up to me and said, 'Here, Mum, I love you too much.' It hit me like lightning. My boy had never done that before – and has never done it again since! It was as if God had sent him. I thought, *If I do this, then he goes through life without his birth mother, and is that history repeating itself? I have to live, for my son.*

I'm a Gamilaroi woman, born in Coonamble, New South Wales, in 1954. As a young child I lived in a camp with my uncles and aunties and cousins. It was a happy camp. My uncles would play the guitar, my grandfather would play the violin, and we had other uncles on the gum leaves and clap sticks. My mum and her sisters had beautiful voices and they would harmonise. I was sung to sleep every night at the campfire. Music filled my life. Life was very simple but to a child, life should be simple and happy and carefree. We would swim in the Castlereagh River and my brothers would go fishing. There were about fifteen cousins. We had one tin shack, which we kids would sleep in, and many tents, which my aunties and uncles slept in. The men would go away rabbit-trapping, setting fences, working with sheep. And so my life was strongly influenced by my mum and aunties. They were homemakers who sang and fed the children.

We always cooked outside. Our diet was mainly kangaroo, sheep and fish. Mum would cook johnnycakes and damper on the fire. We had Sunshine powdered milk, which many families would have had during the Depression – I loved it. If adults spoke, the children were shooed away. They would say, 'No, you go play. Men are talking, women are talking.' We were never allowed to hear the conversations of adults. Now, I wonder whether they were talking about the government taking children away.

When I was five years old my mum received a letter from the government instructing her to have her seven children assembled at the train station in seven days' time. She knew what that letter meant. Families had heard stories from other camps about the white men who took your kids away. You couldn't oppose it. We kids thought we were going for a joyride around the block. Mum never told us what was actually going to happen. She said to my brother, 'Now, you're the eldest, you have to take care of your brothers and sisters.' She went to the op shop and bought us all new clothes. The boys were in little white shirts and black shorts and black bow ties. I was in this dress with oranges and apples and pears on it. I can still visualise it. I'd had my hair brushed. We thought we were pretty fancy, getting all dressed up to go out.

We were taken to the station by an Aboriginal lady who drove a taxi. There were two carloads because there were seven of us children. I was sitting in the back with my brother and I remember looking down at the black shiny shoes I had on. I was clicking my heels and thinking, *Oh, I look really pretty.* Then I noticed Mum wasn't talking, which was odd. Mum was always talking or singing. When we arrived, there were lots of people at the train station. I recall a lot of legs. We were running in and out between them because we were excited. We saw train smoke in the distance and the *toot-toot* sound came. We got on the train and it was all very exciting, and then a white lady came and sat next to me. She had a hat on. I thought, *Why is she sitting next to me? This is Mum's seat.* The train shunted forward. I was sitting opposite my brothers, Barry and Widdy. And I looked out and saw my mum and aunties left behind on the platform.

I pressed my face against the window. Mum had a blue dress on, and she waved her little white hanky and we all cried. I watched Mum waving the hanky and it got smaller and smaller as we moved further away. It was the first time in my life that I ever felt afraid. My brother and I kept asking why Mum wasn't on the train. Barry tried to reassure me. He was nine, and I was five. He said, 'Oh, Mum will be on the next train.' After travelling all night, we arrived in Sydney. My brothers stood up and I began walking off the train with them, when the white lady pulled me back. The white lady said, 'No, you sit here.' Barry protested but my brothers were ushered off. They were put on another train to Kinchella Boys' Home in Kempsey and we were separated.

I arrived in Newcastle on 22 April 1960. As a five-year-old child, you do the right thing and stay with the adult in charge, so I followed the white lady in the hat. Newcastle train station was different to Coonamble because at home we had all these deep, dark-brown legs to wander between. But here? The people all had fair-coloured legs. There was something else too: the shoes. Everyone had fancy shoes. In fact, everyone was *wearing* shoes. That was so different from home because my uncles never wore shoes. I was still watching these shoes when the hat lady came back with a woman and a man. She said, 'Donna, this is your new mummy and daddy. Go with them and they'll give you something to eat.'

I remember sitting in their little Holden and looking out the back window. My foster mum had a beautiful smile but I stayed silent because that's what you do when you're in shock and you don't know what has happened. My foster parents' house was right on the railway track and I kept thinking, *If I walk on that track it will take me back to my camp.* My Aboriginal mum had played the piano accordion around our campfire every night. When I walked into my new home, I saw that my foster mum owned two piano accordions. She has a soprano voice, a very high voice and my Aboriginal mum had a deep alto voice. But they both played piano accordions, so I guess that helped me a bit.

I went from living in a camp with fifteen kids to a European house with two adults who were old enough to be grandparents. We went to church the next week. I liked Sunday School because I saw other kids and I was relieved. They were all white, but at least I could go there and be with other children. I grew up in the church and have always loved it. I remember that I was also given one golliwog and a teddy bear. I used to pretend they were my brothers. I would call them Barry and Widdy and I'd play with them every day. My adoptive dad was home every night and that scared me because I wasn't used to men. In my community they were always away. I was also gagging on the food I wasn't used to: spinach or potatoes or beans. I always thought, *Ugh, ice cream, I'm not going to eat that.* I had to adjust to the food.

I had beautiful foster parents. They adopted me three years later and over the years I began to understand every word they said. They were German and initially spoke their first language to each other and English to me. But eventually I learned. I knew what I was getting for every birthday and Christmas and where Mum was hiding it! I don't think I told my adoptive mum that I understood German until I was about forty years old and she was shocked. My parents showed me through their character and their love that I was always safe. It was a peaceful house. As a child, you think everybody else grows up like you and so I didn't know there was domestic violence in the world until

I was an adult and studying welfare. There was no drinking in my home, no swearing and no violence.

My mum couldn't have children, so she was delighted to have a child. Both my parents were loving. My mum would often say, 'Loyalty is the most important thing for a family.' She would also say, 'Love covers all.' That's what remains with me. Whenever there was a big problem, if I was unhappy in my marriage, or if I was unhappy with Dad, she would say, 'Love covers all.' It was their way of life. As Europeans, my parents were also experiencing racism at the time, so when I started school and the kids started calling me names, they understood what I was going through. There were never any other Aboriginal kids at school. It was just me and all these white kids. But being an only child taught me that I could talk to myself and I could talk to God. I was lonely and I relied on my friendship with God.

It was especially hard because I went to five different primary schools. My parents moved around. By trade, my adoptive father was a butcher but after the war he couldn't cut up any animals because he couldn't stand the sight of blood. When he came out to Australia, he started from the bottom again. People thought that because you've got an accent, you're dumb, so immigrants were given labourer jobs. They started very humbly. My dad would clean people's backyards and take rubbish to the dump and eventually he learned landscape gardening. Dad would paint a house, do it up through landscape gardening, and we'd move on to the next house. We'd do up another house and move again. He was always trying to better himself because both my parents had come from very well-to-do families in Europe.

When I was nine, I started getting angry at my mob for not coming to find me. I was getting older and other kids at school were talking about playing with their cousins and going to their aunties' places for school holidays. It was just Mum, Dad and me in all of Australia. They had no relatives here and that added to my displacement. I had no sense of belonging or identity. And that's exactly what the government wanted, for us to be so confused that we assimilated and became good white kids. It very nearly worked for me. My parents bought a petrol station and when I was a teenager I used to pump petrol before and after school. Being out in society I began to see the reactions from white people when they saw me. White people would say, 'Excuse me, do you mind me asking a question?' and I knew exactly what was coming. They would ask what nationality I was and if I said Aboriginal that was the abrupt end of the conversation. This sort of life experience informs you. You learn what's acceptable to people and what's not – and being Aboriginal was not. I lied because I wanted acceptance.

Throughout my life, there have been many times I've spoken and people have made the most idiotic statements. You don't let how it affects you show on your face but when you drive home you're just crying your heart out and it breaks you. I've always found that on the third day after hearing something awful, I come back fighting, I come back with my power. You need to take time out to process any adversity, to think it through, to work it out. It's like your spirit gets topped up again and you go on.

Everything shifted for me when, aged fifteen, I went to the cinema with my girlfriends and we saw *To Sir, With Love*. All of a sudden, I'm sitting there watching this beautiful Afro-American man, Sidney Poitier, who was so strong and proud. I didn't understand what I was going through at the time, but now when I analyse it, I realise I was watching this proud black man on screen and subconsciously thinking, *If he can do it, I can do it.* That film was so powerful at the time because black people were just dirt. We were at the bottom of the social heap, so to see a black man become a schoolteacher – that just changed my whole life. I had no role models before then, and, in that moment, I saw a future for myself. I went back to the cinema fifteen weeks in a row to see the film again. I even wrote a letter to Sidney Poitier, but he never wrote back.

In European families at the time, it was expected that you would go into the family business, so when I got my leaving certificate around that same age, I started working full-time at my parents' service station. There wasn't a choice of doing anything else. We worked 365 days a year, and one day my husband came in. Well, he wasn't my husband yet. He worked at the dockyards and he pulled in, in his car, for petrol. The first time I served Ron, he and the other boys in the car were jumping around and looking at me and laughing. I was thinking, *I'm fat and dumb and ugly and Aboriginal.* When we started dating six months later, Ron told me, 'The first time I came into the servo and you served me, I fell in love with you at first sight and I said to the boys, "I'm going to marry that girl." And they were laughing, thinking, "Yeah, right."' I wasn't allowed to date until I was seventeen, so Ron waited. We got married in 1973 when I was eighteen.

Ron's dad worked with an Aboriginal man, and they built a big, mountainous road from Armidale to Bellbrook. Ron's grandfather worked with Aboriginal trackers in the national parks. They had a lot of respect for Aboriginal people. If I'd married the wrong person, I wouldn't be who I am today. I'm probably one of only a few hundred Aboriginal women who have never experienced domestic violence. For Aboriginal women who have gone through that, and their children, I would say that we've all got strength, we've all got something there to build upon. Society usually points out all our deficits, but you must always work from a strength-based perspective. Know that each person has a gift, a talent, a strength – and you are one of those people. Even if you come from the most dysfunctional family, you will always have your resilience.

Ron could see I was withdrawing from myself through the years. I'd had my son, Darren, but I still never felt good enough to be Ron's wife. When you don't feel worthy, it reflects on everything. Ron kept saying I needed to find my family, but I didn't want to see them. At fifteen, the welfare office would give you a train ticket, tell you where your mob was, and send you back home. But when I'd turned fifteen I hadn't wanted to go – I was so angry at them for not coming to get me for all those years. Ron finally said, 'I'm saving up so that next year we'll have enough money for petrol, and we can go look for your mum in Coonamble. She might have moved on but at least we've got a starting point.'

Then one day I went to a ladies' meeting. I had tried to get out of it but a beautiful non-Aboriginal friend, Julie, had taken me along with her. There was one other Aboriginal lady there. You had to sign a register going in and I looked for her name: it was Margaret Welsh. My Aboriginal mum's name was Beatrice Margaret Welsh. I thought, *Is that my mum?* I sat there in silence.

Julie said, 'Don, why are you looking at that lady?'

'She's got the same name as my birth mother,' I replied.

I was shy back then, so we waited until morning tea to approach her. At the last minute, after the bell had rung to go back in, I walked up to her. She asked me what my name was.

I told her and she replied, 'Donna, I know who your mother is, because you're the spitting image of her. She's my husband's aunty, and we have been looking for you everywhere.'

I admit that I was a little surprised. I'd been angry all my life for my mob not coming to look for me; I thought they didn't want me. So when the aunty said that, I took it with a grain of salt. I did believe her but I was a little hesitant. I was a very shy person. It took me three days to write to Mum and two days for the letter to reach her. When it did, Mum was in another town. My brother Robbie saw the name 'Donna' on the back of the envelope, so he hitchhiked to Mum. While he usually got a ride pretty quickly, he had to walk 25 kilometres before he got a lift that day. But he delivered that letter.

Mum received the letter on a Saturday, the day before Mother's Day. She waited to open it then, and she cried and cried. She said, 'It's Donna.' Everyone else, all my siblings, had gone home with the welfare office support when they were fifteen. Everyone except me. I was twenty-seven years old when I found my mum again. Mum said it was the best Mother's Day gift she had ever had. Mum and I wrote back and forth, at first only every six months. We were both apprehensive. I was struggling with my identity and didn't understand why she gave me away. We didn't know anything about Stolen Generations back then. As a five-year-old, I had assumed that my family didn't want me. I had also seen all the stereotypes that the media portrayed about Aboriginal people, and how people had treated me when I said I was Aboriginal. I thought the worst of my people.

Mum and I didn't meet until three years later. But when we did, that was the beginning of my healing. I told her she was wearing a blue dress and waving a white hanky when I last saw her, and Mum couldn't believe I remembered. I met all of my brothers and sisters again, and that was wonderful. Nobody said it, but I sensed and felt it: they now saw me as a white person. By that, I mean my values, my attitudes, the way I was raised and the way I spoke, all seemed white to them. Mum still lived in the same town, same street, waiting. She wasn't going to move away until all her children came home. I asked my mum, 'Where was I born? Where did we live near the camp?' She took me over to the next-door neighbours' place and she said, 'See that tree, that's the tree you used to climb.' They had called it Donna's Tree.

With all those years that had passed, it was huge.

When I lost my mum four years later, I realised I didn't know my history the way I should, and so I went to university. Learning my people's history was an awakening that was empowering. That's when I first learned about the Stolen Generations. I thought I was the only one in Newcastle but I was so wrong. I soon became a mouthpiece for the Stolen Generations. The more I share my story, the stronger I get. The more healing that I experience, the more I can open other people's eyes as well, raising white consciousness of what happened to kids like me.

Aboriginal people have always had to get permission to have a voice. When I arrived at university, I had been conditioned by all of that and it was the first institution to give me permission to speak up. Older generations of Aboriginal people have had to learn that, learn that we have a voice, and really the young ones have had to learn too. I've got three boys now. Throughout their teenage years, I was a silent role model. When they saw me go to university, within six months all their grades had come up. As I was learning about my culture, I was talking about it at home so they were listening and learning too. We weren't a political family, we were just trying to survive day by day.

You spend your life trying to work out why people don't like you because of the colour of your skin. Mostly, you can't make sense of it. I can't tell you how many times I've been pushed in front of while in the line at Coles. In the old days, our aunties would say, 'Oh, we knew our place and we'd just be quiet.' After university, I prepared a sentence to use if someone pushed in front of me again at the shops. And do you know what? Once I had that sentence ready to go, it never happened again. Isn't that amazing? It's like there was this neon sign that said, 'Walk all over her,' and when I found my voice, I turned it off.

Life is full of challenges and I wouldn't be who I am today without those experiences. At five, I became an only child, and twenty-one years ago, I became a widow. My husband passed away from lung cancer in 1999 and the strength I got from my childhood was the well that I pulled water from to live through that tragedy. Growing up by myself enabled me to transition to becoming widowed and to cope with sitting alone in a house, making all my own decisions and being independent. Whatever we go through, nothing's ever completely lost. When I talk to young Aboriginal girls I say, 'Give yourself permission. We think we're not worthy, that we don't have anything to contribute to society, but once someone else believes in us, we capture that vision and think, *Okay, if they believe in me then I'll start working on that.*

'We have to learn to love ourselves. Your birthright, your Aboriginality, it's in your blood, it's in your genes, it's your family's inheritance. It can't be bought, it can't be sold, it is yours to embrace. No one can take it from you.'

In 1985, I knelt at my bed and said, 'Lord, I want to be a real Aboriginal, I want to identify with my people, and become one of them.' I believe my life's work has been the answer to that prayer. As doors open, we have to have the courage to walk through them. I never planned to go to university but I've graduated four times now. I've gone back and learned more and more – and the doors have continued to open. I'm now an international author, an Indigenous Chaplain, a radio producer, a public speaker and a switchboard operator.

I think the coronavirus has taught us about everything we've taken for granted – and shown us how to appreciate that. As Aboriginal people we don't have a word for 'hello'. We hug. During this time, we haven't been able to hug people. Of course, this isn't the first virus to be introduced to Australia. When the colonists came they brought influenza and thousands of our people died from the common flu because we'd never had it. We had sat around the campfire burning Eucalyptus leaves all our lives. Then the next boat brought smallpox, and wiped out 8000 Aboriginal men, women and children. Our women were raped and they got syphilis and lupus. All these diseases came from England. We didn't have them here. And so we've had the coronavirus, but there will be another disease, and another, in time.

Seven years after I sent Mum that first letter, she died. We had her funeral on the Saturday, the day before Mother's Day. Her funeral was the first Aboriginal funeral I'd ever gone to and I did everything wrong. I wore lemon-and-white stockings and white shoes. You're meant to wear black and white. I stuck out like a sore thumb. It was one-thirty in the afternoon, and I was sitting in Mum's backyard, just looking around at the people. It was at that moment I had the realisation: this is my mob, this is my people, this is my belonging, this is my identification. And I just started crying. There were about 500 people at the funeral, and they thought I was crying because Mum had gone. I told Aunty Tam what happened, and she said, 'Our elders would say that your mum's spirit just came upon you.'

Mum was the welfare worker of the family. After all seven of her children were taken away, she was the 'Mum Shirl' of Coonamble. She took in all the kids who were on the streets and gave them a feed and a bed for the night. That's the love that she had and that's the love that I felt just after her funeral, sitting in the backyard. Up until that time, I was embarrassed to identify as Aboriginal because of everything I'd experienced. But now, I fell in love with my people. *Everyone* was beautiful. I know the hour and the day that this revelation happened. The day I fell in love. I needed to fall in love with a race of people and, ever since, my work has been in advocating, supporting, praying, and singing that love into their lives.

Donna Meehan is sixty-five years old and lives in Newcastle. Donna shared her story with Emily J. Brooks.

Conclusion

By Helen McCabe, Future Women

*'I can be changed by what happens to me, but
I refuse to be reduced by it.'* – Maya Angelou

The past offers clues to the future, as the lives of these extraordinary women demonstrate. For those living and working in the present, priorities and practices have changed rapidly. Having a job now seems more important than a pay rise. Being in the physical company of friends and family is cherished. No matter how complex it may seem or feel at times, life in the end is quite simple. Having or finding a purpose is what brings meaning, regardless of the global catastrophe raging around us.

The nineteen women in this book prove that personal relationships provide the foundation for navigating life. The value of heartfelt human connection, the type where you talk instead of text, cannot be underestimated. When those relationships are solid, no degree of separation, of distance, of time or even isolation can change the way you feel. The single unifying factor between the past, the present and the future is our human capacity for love. It is the thing that can break us when it fails, and elevates the human spirit to dizzying heights when it succeeds.

The women in this book have each lived through extra-ordinary times. Despite this, it was highly personal events that significantly shaped their lives: the separation from a husband, living far away from family, the death of a child. A prolonged period of global unrest was rendered less significant than the ordinary, and sadly familiar, realities of mental illness, financial disadvantage, family violence, suicide, and loneliness. These women's resilience proves even the most heartbreaking personal events can be survived, and that grief requires patience.

The lesson for each of us, surviving the pandemic of 2020 and most likely beyond, is clear. To future-proof ourselves, we must treasure the people we love and care for, and who love and care for us in return. We must nurture and invest in our communities. By sharing our sadness, we recognise our common humanity. How we band together during these trying times will reveal who we are, as individuals and as a society.

There are unsung heroes in every town and city in Australia. There are women leaving gifts on doorsteps, sewing masks for medical personnel, caring for their grandchildren and cooking lunches for their neighbours. We all know someone who is battling cancer, feeding the homeless, fostering a child, struggling with intergenerational addiction, fighting racism or being beaten down by disadvantage. Perhaps in this period of reflection we will grow our appreciation for the countless selfless acts performed daily in our communities for the betterment and care of others.

Future Women was not immune from the coronavirus freight train. Like businesses everywhere, we farewelled staff, reducing costs; and then headed home, closing the door behind us. Each of us took time to adjust, with some finding it harder than others.

I found myself craving space and would head out twice a day, to catch the sunrise and sunset. I did not take my walks for granted. I greedily scheduled them, building my days around this leisure activity instead of meetings. As the days grew shorter and winter turned parks into puddles, I continued to venture out morning and night, walking to calm the mind and soothe the soul.

Once the immediate fears subsided, real conversations began: between staff, with our writers and members. Why were we so busy? How much money do we really need? Why don't we spend more quality time with our parents and grandparents? This dramatic reset also had us returning to habits of the past, finding passion and optimism in a simpler existence. Some of our team found more time for ourselves and others. Though for many frontline workers, time remains a rare luxury.

Future Women also scaled up our online operation with fast and furious pace. We wanted to create a space where women could come together, to connect, to learn and to lead. Perhaps more than ever before, this world is craving real leadership; the kind of leadership that speaks to our unsettled emotions as well as our worsening economy. At Future Women, we help train, identify and bring together the female leaders of the future – the ones who will guide us through the next moment of global upheaval. The ones who understand that community comes first.

I like to think changes are already underway. Many people have already begun to spend less because we need less. We've become more conscious of our elderly neighbours. We shop locally, we invest in the people around us, and by staying at home we've given the earth a chance to breathe a little. Many are more inclined to give generously, especially to the charities who once depended on big businesses for assistance.

Perhaps our community will also find new respect and loyalty for the companies who have delayed bills, mortgage payments and generally made things easier for those doing it tough. We are more sympathetic to and respectful of nurses, we have learned the true workload of teachers and early childhood educators, and we have a newfound appreciation for essential workers. The majority of whom, I might add, are women. We're reconsidering idle clothes racks, calculating the global wastage from the garment industry and moving towards recycled fabrics and outfits. We're remembering that new doesn't always equal better. We are more aware of the significance of storytellers who capture our history and help us understand ourselves in a way that enlightens and inspires.

Future Women set out to promote the advancement of women. We wanted women to have a voice, regardless of age or race, sexuality, disability or socioeconomic status. More than ever, we recognise the significance of building leaders of the future but also facilitating the friendships that will sustain those leaders. We also acknowledge the value of learning and encourage confidence in women to claim that seat at the table and help shape the future for the better.

We owe an untold debt of gratitude to the nineteen so-called ordinary women in this book. These women have given up their time, opened their hearts and shared their collective wisdom with enormous generosity. We thank them for their compassion, their altruism, their steadfastness and their bravery. We thank them for reminding us of our own untold resilience.

At Future Women, we hope to pay it forward.

Acknowledgements

Untold Resilience is testament to the exceptional journalistic skill, hard work and dedication of its writers. Our thanks to Emily J. Brooks, Ginger Gorman, Emily Joyce, Kate Leaver, Juliet Rieden and Kristine Ziwica. We also acknowledge the powerful contribution of Catherine McGregor, who chose to tell her own story. Our gratitude also goes to Neela Janakiramanan and Susan Moshi, who introduced us to some of our much-loved interview subjects.

Patti Andrews not only lives and breathes the Future Women brand, but brings it to life through her exquisite imagination and artwork – including the cover of this book. The rest of the Future Women team have also put up with our absence, distraction, stress, and late-night panics throughout the creation of this book. We're most grateful for their continued loyalty and commitment to the online community of women we're creating together.

Hugh Marks supported Future Women before anyone even knew what it was. His belief in and guidance of the brand continues, alongside fellow board members Lizzie Young and Arabella Gibson. We would also like to acknowledge the early members of Future Women, who kept faith with us through the early days, the growth phase and through the enormous upheaval of a global pandemic.

Thank you to the team at Penguin Random House, whose professionalism, precision and rather ambitious due dates have kept us on the straight and narrow. Isabelle Yates is an extraordinary publisher, with a tremendous career ahead of her. Lou Ryan and Kate Hoy were early champions of this book and Rebekah Chereshsky created an impressive marketing campaign. Angela Meyer took our messy drafts and turned them into an actual book, with the help of Grayce Arlov and Clive Hebard.

Finally, this work does not exist without the enormous generosity of the women who trusted us, laughed and cried with us, and permitted us to tell their stories. Reaching back into the past is not always a pleasant or easy experience but they each did so willingly and shared their recollections honestly. Their resilience will inspire future generations to survive whatever lies ahead; the great, the glorious, the cruel and the confronting.

Future Women honours the life of Lakshmi Maksay whose story we were privileged to tell. Our untold gratitude goes to her, and also to Liz Coles, Carmel Daveson, Audrey Fernandes-Satar, Lilia Graovac, Be Ha, Colleen Hickman, Dottie Hobson, Dot Hoffman, Jutta Dowdy, Catherine McGregor, Dorothy McRae-McMahon, Donna Meehan, Alice Moshi, Val Reilly, Edith Sheldon, Faye Snaith, Marie Wynn and Phoebe Wynn-Pope.